ENDORSEMENT FOR
EMBRACE THE FLAME

I am eternally grateful for people like Lily Dolan who will take the time and intense study required to do such a thorough word study. Never would I have imagined that the word fire would have so much personal and prophetic meaning. In the age in which we now live, with instant definitions and answers at the tip of our fingers, we have become so accustomed to taking only a quick glance at something and then quickly moving on to the next appealing thing on our media screens. Thank God that we still have faithful followers of Jesus who will pull apart and dissect his word in order to comprehend all that God has for us to learn. His word is still so powerful and Lily reminds us that although God is love, and He gently and tenderly draws us to himself, he is also a God to be reckoned with and deserves to remain in a place of reverence and awe. This second book about the word fire will wake you up to the seriousness of the times in which we live. Thank you Lily for your diligence and obedience to your Heavenly Father for we will all be immensely blessed by it.

—Chaplain Patricia J Lutz

EMBRACE THE FLAME

LILY ALVAREZ DOLAN

EMBRACE THE FLAME

TATE PUBLISHING
AND ENTERPRISES, LLC

Published by Tate Publishing & Enterprises, LLC
127 E. Trade Center Terrace | Mustang, Oklahoma 73064 USA
1.888.361.9473 | www.tatepublishing.com

Tate Publishing is committed to excellence in the publishing industry. The company reflects the philosophy established by the founders, based on Psalm 68:11,
"The Lord gave the word and great was the company of those who published it."

Book design copyright © 2015 by Tate Publishing, LLC. All rights reserved.
Cover design by Joseph Emnace
Interior design by Mary Jean Archival

Published in the United States of America

ISBN: 978-1-63449-932-3
1. Religion / Biblical Studies / New Testament
2. Religion / General
15.03.04

In loving memory of John Dennis Dolan

June 10, 1951–June 15, 2012

He reflected Jesus as bright gold through his baptism by fire.

ACKNOWLEDGMENTS

My heartfelt gratitude is for the precious blood of Jesus Christ spilled on the cross of Calvary to cover the sins of all; for the indwelling presence of the Holy Spirit as promised to those who receive the free gift of salvation through faith in Jesus as the only Son of the Most High God born of a virgin; for the hope of eternity in the presence of the Triune God, who was and is and is to come; for the Word of God the Father that will forever remain as the Way, Truth, and Life.

CONTENTS

LIST OF SCRIPTURES

Hosea 7:6–7 Burning Like Ovens of Fire

Hosea 8:14 Cities Set on Fire

Joel 1:19–20 The Pastures and Trees Devoured by Fire

Joel 2:3–5 The Devouring Fire of the Strong Army

Joel 2:30-32 Wonders of Fire

Amos 1:3–14; 2:1–3, 4–6 The Fire Sent for the Transgressions

Amos 5:6 The Lord Breaks Out Like Fire

Amos 7:4–6 Contend by Fire

Obadiah 17–18 The House on Fire

Micah 1:2–5 Mountains Melting Like Wax

Micah 1:6–7 Hires Burned with Fire

Nahum 1:6 His Fury Poured Out Like Fire

Nahum 3:13–15 The Fire Will Devour

Habakkuk 2:13 Labor in the Fire

Zephaniah 1:18 & 3:8 Devoured by the Fire of Jealousy

Zechariah 2:5 A Wall of Fire

Zechariah 3:1–2 A Brand of Fire

Zechariah 9:1–4 Burned in the Sea

Zechariah 11:1 Doors Open to Fire

Zechariah 12:6 A Torch of Fire

Zechariah 13:8–9 Refined by Fire

Malachi 1:10–11 Useless Fire

Malachi 3:1–3 Abiding in the Refiner's Fire

Matthew 3:11–12 Baptized by the Holy Spirit and Fire

Matthew 13:36–43 A Furnace of Fire

Matthew 17:14–21 Falling Into the Fire

Matthew 18:7–9 Everlasting Fire

Matthew 25:31–34, 41 Prepared Fire

Mark 14:53–54 Peter at the Fire

Luke 9:51–56 Commanding Fire?

Luke 12:49–50 Baptism by Fire

Luke 17:28–30 Raining Fire

John 15:4–8 Branches in the Fire

Acts 2:1–4 Tongues of Fire

Acts 28:1–6 Paul Builds a Fire

1 Corinthians 3:13–15 Revealed by Fire

2 Thessalonians 1:7–10 A Flaming Fire Taking Vengeance

Hebrews 1:7,14 Ministers as Flames of Fire

Hebrews 11:33–34 Fire Quenched by Faith

Hebrews 12:18–24 Mountain Burning with Fire

Hebrews 12:28–29 Our God is a Consuming Fire

James 3:2, 5–6 The Tongue is a Fire

James 5:1–3 Flesh Eaten by Fire

1 Peter 1:7 Tried by Fire

2 Peter 3:7, 11–12 The Heavens on Fire

Jude 7 & 20–23 Pulled Out of the Fire

Revelation 1:12–15; 2:18 & 19:11–13 Eyes as a Flame of Fire

Revelation 3:18 Gold Tried in the Fire

Revelation 4:5 Seven Lamps of Fire

Revelation 8:5 Fire of the Altar

Revelation 8:7 Hail and Fire Mingled with Blood

Revelation 8:8 A Mountain Burning with Fire

Revelation 9:17–18 Breastplates of Fire

Revelation 10:1 Feet as Pillars of Fire

Revelation 11:3–5 Fire From Their Mouth

Revelation 13:13 False Fire

Revelation 14:9–12 Tormented by Fire and Brimstone

Revelation 14:13–20 The Angel with Power Over Fire

Revelation 15:2 A Sea of Glass Mingled with Fire

Revelation 16:8–9 Scorched with Fire

Revelation 17:15–17 & Revelation 18:8 The Whore and Woman
Burned with Fire

Revelation 19:17–21 & Revelation 20:10, 14, 15 & Revelation
21:8 The Lake of Fire

Revelation 20:9 The Final Fire

Song of Solomon 8:6–7 The Eternal Flame

INTRODUCTION

In the summer of 2005, while overlooking a lush aspen forest in Colorado with snowcapped mountains peaks in the distance, I heard the wind rushing through the leaves. It sounded like applause. I understood at that moment what is meant in Isaiah 55:12 to hear the "trees clap their hands." When I read the verses leading up to that one, the Lord gave them to me as a promise for my book.

Beginning in Isaiah 55:8, it reads,

> For my thoughts *are* not your thoughts, neither *are* your ways my ways, saith the Lord. For *as* the heavens are higher than the earth, so are my ways higher than your ways, and my thoughts than your thoughts. For as the rain cometh down and the snow from heaven and returneth not thither, but watereth the earth, and maketh it bring forth and bud, that it may give seed to the sower, and bread to the eater: So shall my word be that goeth forth out of my mouth: it shall not return unto me void, but it shall accomplish that which I please, and it shall prosper *in the thing* whereto I sent it. For ye shall go out with joy, and be led forth with peace: the mountains and the hills shall break forth before

you into singing, and all the trees of the field shall clap *their hands.*

Embrace the Flame is the second book from a personal study of the word fire. It's a continuation of my first book called *Fire in the Bible*. The first book covered Genesis to Daniel. This book covers Hosea to Revelation. My original collection of verses came from *Cruden's Compact Concordance*. I was intrigued to study this word because of some visions of fire the Lord had shown me and because I didn't agree with a teaching that said the baptism of fire was the judgment of hell. I had shared what I was learning with my listeners when I worked as a DJ on a Christian FM station in Tucson, AZ. I later typed my notes and when I retired from radio, I began to research the history and geography surrounding the verses.

My thoughts were to finish the entire study and then present them to a publisher. It was in the fall of 2005 that the Lord led me to do a search online for a Christian publisher, and I submitted my partial manuscript to Tate Publishing. When I received the word that it was accepted, it was exactly three years later to the date I had noted their theme verse in my Bible. Psalm 68:11 says, "The Lord gave the word: great *was* the company of those that published *it.*" I was told that most bookstores want books closer to three hundred pages. It was the Lord's "way" to make this word study two books.

While writing about the fire in the Bible, my husband and I have been going through the fire. That is the main reason it took me so long to finish the first book. While editing it with the publisher, I learned about the discipline of writing. It is not easy for me to sit and focus on one subject for a long time, but every time I did, the Lord would help me to formulate my research as it pertained to each verse. Many times, I would stare at the keyboard without a clue what I would write about, and then several pages later, I sat back in amazement.

In the process of learning about fire in the Bible, I have come to realize that sometimes the word for light in the Bible should have been translated as fire or flame. When we read in Genesis that God spoke light into existence, it was on the first day. The sun, moon, and stars were not created until the fourth day. In using a *Key Word Study Bible* with the *Strong's Dictionary*, I've learned in Hebrew the word for light has the definition of illumination. In Genesis 1:3, the word light is given the number 216 but comes from the root word that means to kindle or set on fire. In translating the verse that says that evening and morning where the first day, I came to the understanding that it essentially means that God covers and uncovers the light/fire. In Job, the oldest manuscript in the Bible, chapter 36, verse 32 says that the Lord covers the light with clouds. In studying the definition of both the words light (216) and clouds (3709), I realized that it could be rendered: The Lord covers the fire with the palm of his hand. The word for clouds in this verse means hollow or palm. The actual word for cloud is numbered 6051.

In researching the Greek, I noticed that in 1 John 1:5 where we learn that God is light, it is given the number 5457 for the Greek word *phos* and also means luminous, fire, or light. There is another word that corresponds to light and that is *luchnos* (3088). In the *Lexical Aid for the New Testament*, I learned that phos is never kindled and therefore never quenched, but luchnos is kindled by another's hands.

We in the modern world see the word light as referring to light from the planets or stars or a light from an electrical source. How could Moses, when writing his first book, express that God spoke light into existence when his only point of reference would be the light of a flame? How could those translating from the original tongues make that difference between light and fire? John 1:4 tells us that in Jesus was life and that life was the light of men. Once again, the word for light in the Greek is phos. That is why the ancient Hebrew manuscript says that in Genesis, where we learn that God breathed the breath of life into Adam and man became a living soul, the word for soul should be fire.

When I submitted my partial manuscript, I had finished Zechariah 2:5 where the Lord said He would be a wall of fire around Jerusalem and the glory in the middle of her. I did not return to Zechariah until after the first book was published in the spring of 2007. I know that was providential. The vision of the Lord in a wall of fire is one of the reasons I was prompted to study the word fire.

I could never have imagined all that the Lord would reveal to me as I have studied the word fire. My books represent only a small percentage of all the verses that speak of fire. However, those that I have studied have helped to "connect the dots" in my understanding of prophecy. I did not begin this word study with the intention of refuting the popular notion of a pre-tribulation rapture, but it became apparent to me in the process. I can understand why it would be difficult to understand the Old Testament prophets, but because they spoke with God's fire, they reveal how important and relevant their messages are to us now. The challenge is to align their prophecies with the New Testament prophecies given by Jesus and His apostles. In doing so, we gain a more complete understanding. In essence, you join me in the learning process. I look forward to what the Holy Spirit will reveal about the fire of God in the New Testament.

When I finished the editing process of the first book in the winter of 2006, I looked up from my desk to the snow-covered mountains outside my home in Tucson, AZ, and remembered God's promise from Isaiah 55. The Lord had given me a word and it was like the snow melting that made this book bud and blossom, not only in the written form but also as an audio book. I believe the word He has given me will not return to Him void. I trust Him to accomplish what He has purposed through sharing it with you. I believe it will go where He intended to send it. I know it will prosper in giving His people understanding about the Holy Fire of Yahweh. With the second book finished, I hold to the verse in Hebrews 10:36 that says, "For ye have need of patience, that, after ye have done the will of God, ye might receive the promise." Learning about fire in the Bible and going through the fire has allowed me to know intimacy with the Triune God within that wall of fire. That is my desire for you as well.

As the Lord leads,
Lily

1

HOSEA

BURNING LIKE OVENS OF FIRE

For they have made ready their heart like an oven, whiles they lie in wait: their baker sleepeth all the night; in the morning it burneth as a flaming fire. They are all hot as an oven, and have devoured their judges; all their kings are fallen: there is none among them that calleth unto me. (Hosea 7:6–7)

The prophet Hosea was a citizen of northern Israel and prophesied at the same time as Isaiah, Amos, and Micah before 749 BC, during the second reign of Jeroboam who was a contemporary of Uzziah, king of Judah. There is a difference of opinion as to whether Hosea actually took back an adulterous wife or that it was only written symbolically. Either way, the story represents God's willingness to forgive Israel, as His bride, for her infidelity, love of foreign gods, and alliances with other nations. The first three chapters tell the story of Hosea's wife and children who are used to represent the Lord's judgment and final restoration in the latter days. Chapters 4–14 are a summary of Hosea's prophetic teaching that are believed to have been compiled at the end of his ministry.

Hosea 4:1 tells us that the reason the Lord has a controversy with the inhabitants of the land is because there is no truth, no mercy, and no knowledge of God.

Probably one of the most familiar verses is found in Hosea 4:6:

> My people are destroyed for lack of knowledge: because thou hast rejected knowledge, I will also reject thee, that thou shalt be no priest to me: seeing thou hast forgotten the law of thy God, I will also forget thy children.

The worship of other gods is considered "whoredoms" and Israel is considered a harlot for adopting the religious practices of the pagan nations around her. Hosea 4:11 reads, "Whoredom and wine and new wine take away the heart." In chapter 5, the Lord declares through Hosea to Israel, Judah, and Ephraim the judgment they will face. In verses 6–7, even though they seek the Lord, He will "withdraw" himself from them because they have "dealt treacherously" with the Lord by producing "strange children" as a result of their intermingling with other nations.

In chapter 6, we read of two other familiar verses. Verses 1–3 read,

> Come, and let us return unto the Lord: for he hath torn, and he will heal us; he hath smitten, and he will bind us up. After two days will he revive us; in the third day he will raise us up, and we shall live in his sight. Then shall we know, *if* we follow on to know the Lord; his going forth is prepared as the morning; and he shall come unto us as the rain, as the latter *and* former rain unto the earth.

In the following verse, the Lord is asking what He can do for Judah and Ephraim because their goodness is "as a morning cloud, and as the morning dew that goes away."

Verses 5–6 read,

> Therefore have I hewed *them* by the prophets; I have slain them by the words of my mouth: and thy judgments *are as* the lights *that* goeth forth. For I desired mercy, and not sacrifice; and the knowledge of God more than burnt offerings.

Unfortunately, we learn in the following verse that they have "transgressed the covenant." Chapter 7 begins by proclaiming that the Lord would have "healed Israel" but they would not admit their wickedness before His face and how their king is glad with their evil and the princes are happy with their lies. Hosea 7:4–8 compares the adulterers and their hearts to an oven that the baker allowed to become a "flaming fire" while he fell asleep. They are like the fire that devours their judges, while the kings fall and no one calls on the Lord. In these verses, we also learn that the baker stops kneading his dough and forgets to turn over the cakes in the oven. Why would the Lord use this analogy to show the people their sin? The comparison of the adultery of Israel with an oven could represent the fire of passions that burns with adultery and the forgetfulness of the baker could represent how this spiritual adultery causes the people to lose their good judgment and forget the Lord who is the "bread of life."

It is not hard to compare the last day's apostate church with Israel during Hosea's time. The adultery of Israel is like the adultery of the modern church that indulges in religious fads that do no align with the word of God.

Ephesians 4:14 warns us:

> That we *henceforth* be no more children, tossed to and fro, and carried about with every wind of doctrine, by the

sleight of men, *and* cunning craftiness, whereby they lie in wait to deceive.

The messages given in these churches are the adulterated word of God and have their beginnings in trying to ally the ways of the world with the word. Be wary of churches that lean on "feelings" in which the service becomes an emotional roller coaster of highs and lows. Adultery is purely based on feelings, not reason, and the end result of those fiery passions leads to the destruction of what was once pure. The letter to the Ephesians in Revelation is to the church that has "left its first love" and that is the adultery of the bride of Christ.

The message in chapter 7 in Hosea ends with these sad swords in verses 13–16:

> Woe unto them! for they have fled from me: destruction unto them! because they have transgressed against me: though I have redeemed them, yet they have spoken lies against me. And they have not cried unto me with their heart, when they howled upon their beds: they assemble themselves for corn and wine, *and* they rebel against me. Though I have bound *and* strengthened their arms, yet do they imagine mischief against me. They return, *but* not to the most High: they are like a deceitful bow: their princes shall fall by the sword for the rage of their tongue: this *shall be* their derision in the land of Egypt.

CITIES SET ON FIRE

> For Israel hath forgotten his Maker, and buildeth temples; and Judah hath multiplied fenced cities: but I will send a fire upon his cities, and it shall devour the palaces thereof. (Hosea 8:14)

This is the last time that the word fire is used in the remaining seven chapters of Hosea. Interestingly, chapter 8 begins with a call to blow the trumpet with a warning that the Lord will come as an eagle against the house of Israel for transgression against His covenant and trespassing His law by establishing kings and princes without the Lord's knowledge and by creating idols from their silver and gold. Many have heard the phrase: "If you sow to the wind, you will reap the whirlwind." Hosea spoke this against Israel in the seventh verse of this chapter. Verse 8 tells us that the Gentiles will swallow up Israel, which describes the dispersion of the Jews. The Lord no longer accepts their sacrifices and declares He will send them back to Egypt in verse 13. The Lord intends to send fire upon the fenced cities to devour the palaces that have been built there. It is glaring to me that even at this time there is a fence that is separating the Jews and the Moslem in Jerusalem. The palaces that exist there are not for the worship of the Most High God.

Beginning in chapter 9, Hosea tells Israel to not rejoice. Their spiritual adultery will take them away from the Lord's land and He will not receive their wine offerings and their sacrifices will be as the "bread of mourners" because the bread for their soul will not be in the house of the Lord according to verse 4. Their corruption will bring about the "days of recompense" as written in verses 7 and 9. Hosea ends this chapter with these words: "My God will cast them away, because they did not hearken unto him: and they shall be wanderers among the nations."

Israel is called an "empty vine" in chapter 10 verse 1 and as having a "divided heart" in verse 2 and verse 3 reads, "For now they shall say, We have no king, because we feared not the Lord; what then should a king do to us?" Verse 8 answers, "The high places also of Aven, the sin of Israel, shall be destroyed: the thorn and the thistle shall come up on their altars; and they shall say to the mountains, Cover us; and to the hills, Fall on us." A similar verse is found in Revelation 6:16 when the sixth seal is opened and men ask the mountains to fall on them to hide them for the wrath of the Lamb. Hosea 10:12 reads, "Sow to yourselves in righteousness, reap in mercy; break up your fallow ground: for *it is* time to seek the Lord, till he come and rain righteousness upon you."

We learn in chapter 11 that God would call His son out of Egypt and this first verse is a reference to Joseph and Mary returning with Jesus as a child to Nazareth after hiding in Egypt while Herod had attempted to destroy the promised king by killing all baby boys in Israel. Here we learn how the love of the Father who tried to heal them and draw them to Himself with the "bands of love" in verses 3 and 4 was demonstrated by sending His Son to deliver His people. Even though verse 7 says that God's people are "bent on backsliding," verse 9 shows the mercy of God and reads, "I will not execute the fierceness of mine anger, I will not return to destroy Ephraim: for I *am* God and not man: the Holy One in the midst of thee; and I will not enter into the city."

Hosea uses the story of Jacob wrestling with the Angel of the Lord in chapter 12 verses 1–6 to tell His people to turn to God, to be merciful, and to use judgment while they wait for the Lord "continually." The remainder of this chapter shows how the Lord uses His prophets in verses 10 and 13 which say, "I have spoken by the prophets, and I have multiplied visions and used similitudes, by the ministry of the prophets...And by a prophet the Lord brought Israel out of Egypt, and by a prophet was he preserved."

Despite the continual sin of Ephraim, the tribe that came from the younger son of Joseph and his Egyptian wife, the Lord declares through Hosea in 13:4, "Yet I *am* the Lord thy God from the land of Egypt, and thou shalt know no god but me: for *there* is no saviour beside me." Hosea concludes in 14:1 with, "O Israel, return unto the Lord thy God; for thou hast fallen by thine iniquity." The unconditional love of God is shown in verse 4 when He says through Hosea, "I will heal their backsliding, I will love them freely: for mine anger is turned away from him." Hosea gives us a beautiful illustration of the Lord being like dew to Israel and causing growth in her like the lily and as an olive tree so that those that rest under his shadow will return and revive. Finally in verse 8, Ephraim turns from their idol worship and we read in verse 9, "Who *is* wise, and he shall understand these *things?* Prudent, and he shall know them? for the ways of the Lord *are* right, and the just shall walk in them: but the transgressors shall fall therein."

Hosea spoke to the people of his time as well as ours. The offerings and sacrifices of an adulterous, backsliding church cannot be accepted by the Holy One of Israel, yet through His love and mercy we can be forgiven by turning away from the idols of this world. We, who believe in Jesus as our Savior but came out of the world, are like Ephraim, Joseph's son, who know of the one true God from but lived in a pagan culture. Take to heart the words of Hosea, let us be wise and prudent, understanding the ways of the Lord and continue to walk in them.

2

JOEL

O Lord, to thee will I cry: for the fire hath devoured the pastures of the wilderness, and the flame hath burned all the trees of the field. The beasts of the field cry also unto thee: for the rivers of waters are dried up, and the fire hath devoured the pastures of the wilderness. (Joel 1:19–20)

There is no actual history of the prophet Joel and the time frame in which he wrote are surmised by the placement of his prophecies after Hosea in the canon of the minor prophecies. Joel speaks of the scattering of Israel, not in reference to the ten tribes but to the descendants of Abraham, Isaac, and Jacob. He did not write during the exile because there is mention of the temple and its service. He probably wrote during the time of Ahaz but before the ministry of Amos during the reign of Uzziah. Joel's prophecies address two main issues. The first is judgment with a call to repentance and prayer. The second is the promise of blessings that follow repentance.

The book begins with scenes of devastation that has been caused by a plague of locusts, which has been made worse because of a drought. The imagery could have resulted from an actual occurrence; nevertheless, it symbolically represents an invading army.

The time for the fulfillment of this prophecy is clear as we read in Joel 1:15, "Alas for the day! for the day of the Lord *is at* hand, and as a destruction from the Almighty shall it come." Revelation 9:3–11 describes the locusts that are released on earth when the bottomless pit is opened at the sounding of the fifth trumpet. However, these locusts do not harm the grass, trees, or those who have the seal of God in their foreheads. They do torment the men on earth for five months so much so that they desire to die but cannot.

So how is it that Joel proclaims that the fire has destroyed the pastures and the trees in chapter 1 verses 19–20? The answers are found in chapter 2 as we read of the strong nation that comes to the inhabitants of the land in verse 2. Notice Joel 1:6 tells of the strong nation that comes against his land, like a strong lion whose army is so large it can't be counted. This army has the appearance of horses and we read that it is the Lord's army in chapter 2 verses 4 and 11.

Joel 2 begins with the well-known verse that reads,

> Blow ye the trumpet in Zion, and sound the alarm in my holy mountain: let all the inhabitants of the land tremble for the day of the Lord cometh, for *it is* nigh at hand: A day of darkness and of gloominess, a day of clouds and of thick darkness, as the morning spreading upon the mountains…

The rest of the verse goes on to describe this great army unlike any that has ever been seen before. Obadiah 17 and Joel 2:32 are similar in that the both speak of the deliverance in mount Zion for the remnant that the Lord will call. Jesus told us that "our redemption is nigh" when we see the desolation of Jerusalem. The fire that goes out before this army causes this desolation and is the subject covered in the next section.

> A fire devoureth before them; and behind them a flame burneth: the land *is* as the garden of Eden before them, and behind them a desolate wilderness; yea, and nothing shall escape them. The appearance of them *is* as the appearance of horses; and as horsemen, so shall they run. Like the noise of chariots on the tops of mountains shall they leap, like the noise of a flame of fire the devoureth that stubble, as a strong people set in battle array. (Joel 2:3–5)

This army is led by the Lord as we read in verse 11, "And the Lord shall utter his voice before his army: for his camp *is* very great: for *he is* strong that executeth his word: for the day of the Lord *is* great and very terrible; and who can abide it?" Revelation 6:17 asks a similar question, "For the great day of his wrath is come; and who shall be able to stand?" This occurs after the sixth seal is opened and the sun is darkened and the moon looks like blood and the stars fall and there is a great earthquake. Notice in Joel 2:10 as the people on earth are in fear of this army we read, "The earth shall quake before them; the heavens shall tremble: the sun and the moon shall be dark, and the stars shall withdraw their shining."

In the previous study when we learned about the locust that are released from the bottomless pit in Revelation 9:1–12, we read in verse 11 that they have a king over them whose name in Hebrew is Abaddon or in Greek is Apollyon meaning "destroyer" and is called the "angel of the bottomless pit." Verse 12 explains that this is the first of two woes when these locusts torment the people on earth. In Revelation 9:12–21 we hear of the army of horsemen that number "two hundred thousand thousand" that are released when the sixth trumpet is blown. Fire and brimstone goes out of their mouth and these horsemen kill a third part of the men. In verses 20–21, we read that the rest of the men that weren't killed by these "plagues" did not stop making and worshipping idols neither did they repent of murder, sorcery, fornication, and thefts.

Just as many who are unfamiliar with the Bible have the mistaken notion that Satan has dominion in hell; likewise, I believe that many have the wrong idea that this angel of the bottomless pit whose name means "destroyer" is in league with Satan. I refer to the event that occurred in 1 Chronicles 21 when David sees the angel that was sent to destroy Jerusalem because of his pride and disobedience in numbering the people after a battle. Verse 15 reads,

> And God sent an angel unto Jerusalem to destroy it: an as he was destroying, the Lord beheld, and he repented him of the evil and said to the angel that destroyed, It is enough, stay now thine hand. And the angel of the Lord stood by the threshingfloor of Ornan the Jebusite.

It was on this site that David built an altar, where his sacrifice was consumed by fire from heaven, and later gave it to Solomon to build the temple on. It is also called Mount Moriah, the site on which Abraham was going to sacrifice his son Isaac in obedience until the Lord provided the ram.

Today, the Moslems worship there in the Dome of the Rock with the permission of the Jews despite having regained the site after the Six-Day War in 1967. Why is this information relevant to this army of horsemen that destroys with fire? First of all, there will come a desolation in Jerusalem for the abominations that occur there when the Antichrist seeks to be worshipped above the Most High God in the temple. This temple has yet to be built. The desolation will be by the hand of Lord of Hosts. It will come to purge this site for building of the millennial temple. Notice in Daniel 9:27, we first read that the sacrifice and oblation will cease.

Joel cries out in chapter 1 verse 13,

> Gird yourselves, and lament, ye priest: howl, ye ministers of the altar: come lie all night in sackcloth, ye ministers of my God: for the meat offering and the drink offering is withholden for the house of your God.

Verses 14–15 are a call for a fast and solemn assembly because the "day of the Lord *is* at hand, and as a destruction from the Almighty shall it come."

Joel follows his warning of this destruction with a plea in chapter 2 verses 12–14,

> Therefore also now, saith the Lord, turn ye *even* to me with all your heart, and with fasting, and with weeping, and with mourning: And rend your heart, and not your garments, and turn unto the Lord your God: for he is gracious and merciful, slow to anger, and of great kindness, and repenteth him of the evil. Who knoweth if he will return and repent, and leave a blessing behind him; *even* a meat offering and a drink offering unto the Lord your God?

It astounds me that when men see these tormenting locusts and then this army of horsemen who devour with fire, they still refuse to repent of their evil. At that time, only one third of the men are destroyed. When David saw the angel of the Lord withdraw His sword, it was because the Lord repented of the evil. Even during the time of the trumpets being blown, as a warning before the bowls of wrath are poured out in Revelation, God is holding back from complete destruction so that some would turn to Him.

> And I will shew wonders in the heavens and in the earth, blood, and fire and pillars of smoke. The sun shall be tuned into darkness, and the moon into blood, before the great and the terrible day of the Lord come. And it shall come to pass, *that* whosoever shall call on the name of the Lord shall be delivered: for in mount Zion and in Jerusalem shall be deliverance, as the Lord hath said, and in the remnant who the Lord shall call. (Joel 2:30–32)

In this last section of the prophecies of Joel surrounding this verse and beginning with Joel 2:15 through 3:21, we are taken to the time of the latter rain referred to in 2:23. The pouring out of the Holy Spirit is often referred to as the latter rain. It's as if, God knowing the trials His church would face before the Lord's return, would send His Spirit in great measure. One of the first indications that this section of prophecy refers to the return of the Lord is found in chapter 2 verse 20 when we see that the "northern army" is removed far away from the Lord's people. After this, the Lord will restore what was destroyed by the locust, cankerworm, palmerworm, and the great army that the Lord said He had sent among His people according to chapter 2 verse 25. This proves that the destruction came by the enemy, by pestilence and by the hand of God.

Some do not believe that there will be destruction in Jerusalem before the Lord returns but this indicates that there will be. The pouring out of His Spirit is after this destruction, then comes restoration as we read in chapter 2 verse 28, "And it shall come to pass *afterward that* I will pour out my spirit upon all flesh…" and goes on to tell of the dreams, visions, and prophecies that will be given. I have heard that the former rain is considered to be the pouring out of the Holy Spirit since the Day of Pentecost in Acts 2. The latter rain will be that pouring out of the Holy Spirit right before the return of the Lord. I believe it will be for those believers that will suffer the same type of persecution that the early church suffered after they received the "power from on high."

The darkening of the sun and the redness of the moon will bear witness that this is the time before the Lord returns according to Joel 2:31. The wonders in the heavens and earth that will accompany these signs are said to be blood and fire, and pillars of smoke according to verse 30. These events are written of in Revelation 6:12, where we read of the sun becoming "black as sackcloth and the moon as blood" and in chapter 8 verses 4 to 7, where the prayers of the saints go up before the throne of God as the "smoke of incense and hail and fire mingled with blood" are cast upon the earth. It is essential to note that these events occur between the opening of the sixth and seventh seal and the blowing of the first trumpet. It is no coincidence that Joel says twice to "Blow the trumpet in Zion" in chapter 2 verse 1 to sound the alarm on God's holy mountain because the day of the Lord is close and in chapter 2 verse 15 to sanctify a fast and to call a solemn assembly. The opening of the sixth seal is the "great day of the wrath of the Lamb." Before the seventh seal is opened, we read of the 144,000 of the tribes of Israel being sealed for protection and the gathering of all tribes, nations, and tongues before the throne in heaven in Revelation 7. I believe all these things happen simultaneously.

The opening of the seventh seal in Revelation 8 is marked by a half hour of silence and the vision of the angels of the seven trumpets. I believe the silence is the prayers of the saints being heard before the throne of God before the smoke goes up from the incense. Before the trumpets are blown, the censer filled with fire from the altar is thrown down to earth causing voices, thunderings, and lightnings, and an earthquake. We read of the voices, thunderings and lightnings when John first sees the heavens opened and this proceeds from the throne of God in Revelation 4:5 and again in Revelation 11:19 when the temple of God was opened in heaven after the seventh trumpet is blown and the nations were angry because of the wrath of God had come. Notice that when John sees the vision in chapter 4 verse 1 that the voice is like a trumpet. This voice like a trumpet is also in Revelation 1:10 and verse 11 explains that it says, "I am Alpha and Omega, the first and the last." This is when John starts writing to the seven churches. John wrote in verse 10 that he "was in the spirit on the Lord's day." Could this mean all that John saw was written from the perspective of the Lord's day or in other words "the day of the Lord?"

We limit our understanding to think of everything in the book of Revelation occurring in a chronological order or by are own reasoning. If John was in the spirit, he was seeing and hearing outside of a natural understanding of time and space, it was a supernatural experience that cannot be confined to our limited senses.

Have you ever considered that the letters to the seven churches were written to help the body of Christ, His Church, endure the tribulation? When I think of the great and terrible day of the Lord, I think of how we have forgotten the fear of the Lord. With a comfortable Christianity and a skate into heaven mentality, what would we do if we faced persecution like the early church? Could we endure being stoned or beheaded or burned? Many believe we will be raptured out of having to face tribulation, but Jesus said we would see these things—the wars, earthquakes and famines, the sun and moon being darkened before that day. Second Thessalonians 2:3–4 tells us that the apostasy will occur before the Antichrist will be revealed and that won't happen until he tries to be worshipped in the temple. Even though those who believe in a pre-tribulation rapture maintain that we should not be looking for the Antichrist, imagine how they could lose faith or "fall away" if they find they are living at that time.

The third chapter of Joel tells of the time in the "valley of decision." The Lord will gather all nations there in the valley of

Jehoshaphat because they have "parted his land," scattered and sold His people and taken His silver and gold according to the first five verses. It is a time when the Lord gathers the heathen to judge them. Consider that even now the United Nations is planning to create a Palestinian state by parting the land between the Moslems and Jews. Verse 13 talks about the harvest that is ripe and the wine press that overflows with wickedness. I believe this is what is written of in Revelation 14:14–20 when there is the harvest on earth and then the gathering of the clusters of grapes for the "great winepress of the wrath of God." This is before the seven bowls of wrath are poured out. The day in the valley of decision is the day when the sun and moon are darkened according to Joel 3:14–15, again called the day of the Lord. Despite the heavens and earth being shaken when the Lord "roars out of Zion" in verse 16, we learn that the Lord will be "the hope of his people, and the strength of the children of Israel." The book ends with the promise of the "fountain of the Lord" coming out of His house which is also referred to in Zechariah 13:1 which will cleanse the "house of David."

However, we read in Joel 3:19, Egypt and Edom will be a desolation for the innocent blood of Judah that was shed by them. In verse 21, the Lord speaks through Joel when He says, "For I will cleanse their blood *that* I have not cleansed: for the Lord dwelleth in Zion. This is a cleansing for the Jews as they recognize Jesus as Messiah, and at the same time, they recognize the Antichrist is in their temple wanting to be worshipped above the Most High God. This is the moment they are sealed and also the same time as the great day of the Lord's wrath. On Mount Zion, deliverance shall come to the remnant the Lord will call. We read of this remnant, the 144,000 on Mount Zion in Revelation 14:1, and in verses 6–7, we learn of the angel that preaches the "everlasting gospel" to all nations, tribes, and tongues on earth telling them to "Fear God, and give glory to him; for the hour of his judgment is come and worship him that made heaven and earth, and the sea, and the fountains of water." This is before the harvest of believers by the Son of man on the cloud in Revelation 14:14–16 and the gathering by another angel with the sickle of the wicked grapes for the winepress of the wrath of God in Revelation 14:17–20.

The harvest by the Lord is of those who come as a result of the pouring out of the "latter rain." They are the ones who endure the part of the tribulation before the wrath of God is poured out. They are the ones who are tried and made white as the prophet Daniel spoke of in 11:35. They are those of understanding who know their God in Daniel 11:32 that are strong and do exploits and instruct many. They are the ones who have the "patience of the saints" who are overcome for forty-two months in a war with the beast that rises out of the sea in Revelation 13:1–10. They are the ones who do not receive the mark of the beast and are beheaded for their testimony and witness of Jesus according to Revelation 20:4 and they live and reign with Christ in the millennium. Joel understood the meaning of "Blowing the trumpet in Zion" just as Matthew did when he wrote in 24:31, "And he shall send his angels with a great sound of a trumpet, and they shall gather together his elect from the four winds, from one end of heaven to the other." His elect are those being gathered from the earth (four winds) and from heaven. Hebrew 12:22 describes Mount Zion as the city of the living God, the heavenly Jerusalem. This is from where the trumpet will be blown.

In Joel 2:15–16, when the command goes out to "Blow the trumpet in Zion," we read, "Gather the people, sanctify the congregation, assemble the elders, gather the children, and those that suck the breasts: let the bridegroom go forth of his chamber, and the bride out of her closet." This is symbolic of the Lord coming for His church. Traditionally for the Jews, the expectation of the bridegroom coming for his bride was at the Feast of Pentecost. This celebration was also known as the Feast of Weeks because the number seven connected it to the cycle of religious feast. The date was set seven full weeks after the firstfruits of the harvest were presented on the day after that final Sabbath which adds up to fifty days and so the name Pentecost. We wait for the final week of Daniel's seventy weeks of years when the firstfruits of the harvest will be reaped when the Son of Man comes for His bride, those faithful to Jesus Christ.

3

AMOS

Thus saith the Lord; for three transgressions of Damascus, and for four, I will not turn away *the punishment* thereof; because they have threshed Gilead with threshing instruments of iron: But I will send a fire into the house of Hazael, which shall devour the palaces of Ben-hadad. I will break also the bar of Damascus, and cut off the inhabitant from the plain of Aven, and him that holdeth the sceptre from the house of Eden: and the people of Syria shall go into captivity unto Kir, saith Lord. Thus saith the Lord; For three transgressions of Gaza, and for four, I will not turn away *the punishment* thereof; because they carried away captive the whole captivity, to deliver *them* to Edom: But I will send a fire on the wall of Gaza, which shall devour the palaces thereof: and I will cut off the inhabitant from Ashdod, and him that holdeth the sceptre from Ashkelon, and I will turn mine hand against Ekron: and the remnant of the Philistines shall perish, saith the

Lord God. Thus saith the Lord; For three transgressions of Tyrus, and for four, I will not turn away *the punishment* thereof; because they delivered up the whole captivity to Edom, and remembered not the brotherly covenant: But I will send a fire on the wall of Tyrus, which shall devour the palaces thereof. Thus said the Lord; For three transgressions of Edom, and for four, I will not turn away *the punishment* thereof; because he did pursue his brother with the sword, and did cast off all pity, and his anger did tear perpetually, and he kept his wrath for ever: But I will send a fire upon Teman, which shall devour the palaces of Bozrah. Thus saith the Lord; For three transgressions of the children of Ammon, and for four, I will not turn away *the punishment* thereof; because they have ripped up the women with child of Gilead, that they might enlarge their border: But I will kindle a fire in the wall of Rabbah, and it shall devour the palaces thereof, with shouting in the day of battle, with a tempest in the day of the whirlwind: And their king shall go into captivity, he and his princes together, saith Lord.

Thus saith the Lord; For three transgressions of Moab, and for four, I will not turn away *the punishment* thereof; because he burned the bones of the king of Edom into lime: But I will send a fire upon Moab, and it shall devour the palaces of Kerioth: and Moab shall die with tumult, with shouting *and* with the trumpet: And I will cut off the judge from the midst thereof, and will slay all the princes thereof with him, saith the Lord. Thus saith the Lord; For three transgressions of Judah, and for four, I will not turn away *the punishment* thereof; because they have despised the law of the Lord, and have not kept his commandments, and their lies caused them to err, after the which their father have walked: But I will send a fire upon Judah, and it shall devour the palaces of Jerusalem. Thus saith the Lord; For three transgressions of Israel, and for four, I will not turn away the punishment thereof; because they sold the righteous for silver and the poor for a pair of shoes. (Amos 1:3–15; 2:1–6)

The book of Amos begins by telling us that he is a shepherd in the land of Tekoa, which is in the territory of the tribe of Judah. He prophesied to the ten tribes of Israel during the reign of Uzziah, the king of Judah, and during the reign of Jeroboam, who was the son of Joash, the king of Israel. He prophesied against the idol worship in Bethel, which was an alternative place of worship to Jerusalem when the twelve tribes where split into the northern and southern kingdoms. Amaziah was a king in the northern kingdom that continued the worship of the two golden calves in Bethel that were set up by Jeroboam I.

The repetitive style that Amos used in the first two chapters is meant to strongly demonstrate the judgment of the Lord. However, the first six nations that will be judged by the fire being sent either on the city or the wall of the city are all heathen nations surrounding Israel and Judah. In the beginning of chapter 2, the focus turns to judgment against those who know the one true God, Judah in the south and Israel in the north. It's as if the Lord was trying to say that if He would bring this judgment against the heathen nations, how much more so against Judah and Israel. Although Israel is mentioned as having committed transgressions, we do not read of the judgment of fire being sent in the second chapter. What is prophesied against Israel in the remainder of chapter 2 basically gives the impression that they will be weakened in battle so that they runaway. Amos speaks directly to the northern kingdom of Israel in chapters 3–9.

There is a specific intent for the wording in the book of Amos as he speaks for the Lord and says, "For three transgressions and for four…" and that is to let us know that if three transgressions weren't enough yet they compounded the anger of the Lord by continuing in their sin. The fire of the Lord is used to demonstrate His righteous anger against iniquity. All of these judgments are pronounced after we read in Amos 1:2, "The Lord will roar from Zion, and utter his voice from Jerusalem; and the habitations of the shepherds shall mourn, and the top of Carmel shall wither." So these judgments will occur when the Lord roars from Zion. Jesus is called the Lion from the tribe of Judah. Joel 3:16 tells of the time that the heavens and earth will shake when the Lord will roar out of Zion. Revelation 10:1–3 describes the angel that cried like a lion roaring who stood upon the earth and the sea. When he cried, seven thunders spoke but in verse 4 John is told not to write what he hears. According to Revelation 10:6–7, this is at the time when the seventh angel sounds his trumpet and we are told, "there should be time no longer" and that the "mystery of God should be finished, as he hath declared to his servants the prophets." Amos was a servant to God as His prophet who boldly spoke the warnings of the judgments of fire to come.

THE LORD BREAKS OUT LIKE FIRE

Seek the Lord, and ye shall live; lest he break out like fire in the house of Joseph and devour it, and *there be* none to quench *it* in Bethel. (Amos 5:6)

This prophecy was directed specifically to the house of Joseph, which refers to the tribes of Manasseh and Ephraim who occupied the territory surrounding Bethel. Bethel had been established as an alternative place of worship for the ten tribes of Israel when they had broken away from the twelve. It was feared by the priests in the northern kingdom of Israel that the people would defect if they were to travel to Jerusalem to worship with Judah and Benjamin in the southern kingdom. Amos prophesied boldly against the idol worship of the two golden calves in Bethel and that is why the beginning of the above prophecy says in Amos 5:4–5,

For thus saith the Lord unto the house of Israel, Seek ye
me, and ye shall live: but seek not Bethel, nor enter into
Gilgal, and pass not to Beersheba: for Gilgal shall surely
go into captivity, and Bethel shall come to nought.

These words precede the judgment of fire against Joseph.

In the rest of the chapter that follow, Amos addresses the fact that the virgin of Israel had fallen and that she no longer served God but idols. He also says they hated the one that rebukes at the gate and abhors the one that speaks uprightly. He warns them to "hate the evil and love the good and to establish judgment in the gate: because it may be that the Lord, God of host will be gracious unto the remnant of Joseph." Finally he tells them to "let judgment run down as waters and righteousness as a mighty stream."

In Amos 5:10, when we read, "They hate him that rebuketh in the gate, and they abhor him that speaketh uprightly," I am reminded of the word "gatekeepers" used in a class I took on broadcast news. They are the ones in the news media or government who are responsible for what news is or is not released to the public. I think of how it is difficult to trust the media because of the inherent bias in individuals and the agenda of news agencies. It is true of the media today that gives a biased, negative slant to news about Christians and Jews.

In this passage, it talks of those "in the gate" who Amos says tried to speak truth, righteousness, and judgment, yet are hated for it. The prophets spoke at the gate before the people entered the temple to warn the people. At the same time, it could be said of the churches that speak "smooth" words rather than the truth, so that they might tickle ears, meaning they tell the people what they want to hear rather than what they need to hear. The end result is that the congregation ends up being "tossed to and fro" by every wind of doctrine.

Over more than twenty years of walking with the Lord, I have seen many fads take hold in the church. In the mid-eighties, there was an intense emphasis on spiritual warfare to an unscriptural level because of some fictional books by a Christian on that subject. Some Christians and churches have used a series of books based on a pre-tribulation rapture as if it were the only way to view the subject. This is the personal agenda of the authors who belong to an institution, which takes that stance. How is it that so many in the church could turn to these "understandings of men" and take it for truth even if they are fictional rather than seeking the Word of God for understanding? How different is the church today than at the time of Amos when they accepted the worship of golden calves as a substitute for the worship of the one true God of Israel?

It is no wonder when Amos spoke for the Lord, we read in chapter 5 verses 21–23,

> I hate, I despise your feast days, and I will not smell in your solemn assemblies. Though ye offer me burnt offerings, and your meat offerings, I will not accept *them*: neither will I regard the peace offering of your fat beasts. Take thou away from me the noise of thy songs; for I will not hear the melody of thy viols.

The most powerful verses in this fifth chapter are found in verses 18–20:

> Woe unto you that desire the day of the Lord! to what end *is* it for you? the day of the Lord *is* darkness, and not light. As if a man did flee from lion, and a bear met him; or went into the house, and leaned his hand on the wall, and a serpent bit him. *Shall* not the day of the Lord *be* darkness, and not light? even very dark, and no brightness in it?

If Amos would speak this warning twice, we need to understand the seriousness of what the day of the Lord will really be like as opposed to what the current trend of thinking is based on a fictional account of the last days.

Amos says to seek good and not evil so that we might live and that the Lord, the God of hosts will be with us in chapter 5 verse 14. God gives a warning and then shows how to avoid judgment. The fifth chapter ends with the warning that Joseph will go into captivity because they continue to worship the idols that they have made for themselves. The notions of men are the idols that they make for themselves today and the attention that is given them are the sacrifices that the Lord will not receive. He knows that the rebellious and proud will not seek Him so their judgment ultimately will bring eternal captivity in the lake of fire.

CONTEND BY FIRE

> Thus hath the Lord God shewed unto me: and, behold, the Lord God called to contend by fire, and it devoured the great deep, and did eat up a part. Then said I, O Lord God, cease, I beseech thee: by whom shall Jacob arise? for he *is* small. The Lord repented for this: This also shall not be saith the Lord God. thus he showed me and behold the Lord stood upon a wall *made* by a plumbline with a plumbline in his hand. (Amos 7:4–6)

This is one of three visions that Amos is shown in chapter 7 which followed God's warning to all of those who are at ease and are not grieved for the affliction of Joseph in chapter 6. It is in chapter 6 verse 8 that we read of the Lord saying through Amos, "I abhor the excellency of Jacob, and hate his palaces: therefore will I deliver up the city with all that is therein." So when Amos begins in chapter 7 with the vision of the destruction of the harvest by grasshoppers, the Lord repents upon the pleading of Amos in verse 1–3. These two visions are within the group of five that Amos sees in the remaining chapters that include the vision of the plumb line, the basket of summer fruit, and of the Lord standing beside the altar. In the final three visions, Amos does not plead for Jacob as in the first two. When he delivers the vision of the plumb line in verses 7–9, in which the Lord promises desolation and judgment, Amaziah, the priest of Bethel, tells him in 7:13 to not prophesy there anymore and told Jeroboam, king of Israel, that Amos was conspiring against him.

Next, Amos explains that he was not a prophet or a prophet's son but a herdsman when the Lord called him to speak to the nation of Israel. Because the priest had told Amos not to speak against Israel or Isaac, the Lord proclaimed in verse 17,

> Therefore thus saith the Lord, Thy wife shall be an harlot in the city, and thy sons and thy daughters shall fall by the sword, and thy land shall be divided by line; and thou shall die in a polluted land: and Israel shall surely go into captivity forth of his land.

Amos prophesied during the reigns of Uzziah and Jeroboam about 790 BC until about 750 BC. The fall of Israel by Sargon occurred about 721 BC and the invasion of Judah around 714 BC. The prophecy against the northern kingdom by Amos came about seventy years later.

The eighth chapter of Amos describes the vision of the basket of summer fruit that symbolizes that Israel is ripe for judgment. Verse 2 ends with these words to Amos from the Lord, "The end is come upon my people of Israel: I will not again pass by them any more." In the vision of the plumb line, the same phrase was used in chapter 7 verse 8, "I will set a plumbline in the midst of my people Israel: I will not again pass them any more." In Amos 8:3–10, we see the image of the dead in the temple when the songs are turned into "howlings" because of the violence done to the poor. We also read that the land will tremble and rise up as a flood and be thrown down and consumed when the Lord makes the sun go down at noon and the earth dark on a clear day. Verses 11–12 tell of a famine not of food but of hearing the words of the Lord.

The final vision is of the Lord standing by the altar in Bethel commanding to "smite and slay" in chapter 9 as the judgment begins with no escape for the idolaters in verses 1–4. Then we read of the earth melting in the presence of the Lord when He touches the land and how all will mourn as Amos describes the power of the Lord in verses 5–6. Verse 8 proclaims, "Behold, the eyes of the Lord God *are* upon the sinful kingdom, and I will destroy it from off the face off the earth; saying that I will not utterly destroy the house of Jacob, saith the Lord."

It is evident to me that at the pleading of Amos, the Lord relented from completely destroying the land and the people. The names of Jacob and Israel are used interchangeably to refer to the northern kingdom. Amos was from Judah, the southern kingdom. In chapter 9 verses 9–10, we learn that the Lord will "sift the house of Israel among all the nations," but "not the least grain will fall upon the earth," while all of the sinners who say, "the evil will not overtake us or prevent us," will die by the sword. This final chapter ends with the promise that the Lord will raise up the tabernacle of David in that day and rebuild the ruins as it was before when He brings back the captivity of His people to Israel to rebuild the wasted cities where they will live and plant their vineyards to enjoy their own wine never to leave the land again.

If the Lord would say through Amos that he would not pass over His people again, we know that the prophecies have yet to be fulfilled. The power of the Lord being shown in the elements is written of in Revelation as the Lord comes to "sift His people from the nations." I believe this is another way of looking at the rapture because those who accept Christ as Messiah are "engrafted" into the vine, which is Israel. Amos 9:12 declares, after the Lord rebuilds the temple, that Jacob will "possess the remnant of Edom, and of all the heathen, which are called by my name, saith the Lord that doeth this." The provision for those not born of Hebrew descent to be included as those, which are called by His name, is found in that verse.

It is the Lord that will rebuild the temple in the day that He comes back to reign during the millennium. Just as Amos spoke to those who set up the alternative temple in Bethel and practiced the idol worship of Jeroboam I and II, the Lord speaks to us in these days that He will not tolerate adultery in His church, neither will He allow the ultimate blasphemy of the Antichrist in His temple in the last days.

4

OBADIAH

But upon mount Zion shall be deliverance, and there shall
be holiness; and the house of Jacob shall possess their
possessions. And the house of Jacob shall be a fire, and the
house of Joseph a flame, and the house of Esau for stubble,
and they shall kindle in them, and devour them; and there
shall not be any remaining of the house of Esau; for the
Lord has spoken it. (Obadiah 17–18)

The message of Obadiah is addressed to Edom, the descendants
of Esau, and condemns their indifference to their brother Israel
at the time of Babylonian captivity. Psalm 137:7 is a reference
to Edom crying out for the destruction of Jerusalem when it
reads, "Remember, O Lord, the children of Edom in the day
of Jerusalem; who said, Rase *it*, Rase *it*, *even* to the foundation
thereof." This Psalm opens up with: By the rivers of Babylon, there
we sat down, yea, we wept, when we remembered Zion. Jerusalem

was invaded and razed to the ground by Nebuchadnezzar in 587. Jeremiah 49:7–22 and Ezekiel 25:12–14 and chapter 35 contain prophecies for the destruction of Edom for being on the side of Jerusalem's enemies while Israel suffered Babylonian captivity. Second Chronicles 28:17 tells of the history of Edom's betrayal by invading Judah and carrying away captives when Ahaz was king and 2 Kings 16 relates the story of the alliance that Ahaz made with the Assyrians to deliver him in his battle against Syria.

Obadiah begins by saying this is his vision in the first two verses. Then what the Lord God said concerning Edom is called a "rumor." It's about an ambassador that is sent among the heathen who tells them to rise up in battle because the Lord has made them "small among the heathen and greatly despised." Their pride deceives their heart as they claim to be invincible when the Lord declares that He will bring them down in the following verses. Verse 6 tells that all the hidden things of Esau will be searched out. In verses 7–9, they will find those in their confederacy will deceive them and prevail against them. Then the Lord asks if He should destroy the wise and understanding out of Edom to the point that all the mighty ones will be dismayed "to the end that everyone of the mount of Esau may be cut off by slaughter."

Verses 10–14 describe all that the descendants of Esau did against the descendants of Jacob. They rejoiced and behaved proudly as they watched and even helped the Babylonians, as Jerusalem was carried away captive as if they were strangers. Yet Obadiah gives this word a future application when he declares in verses 15–16 when the "day of the Lord comes," all they have done to Jacob will happen to them and deliverance will come to Zion because the house of Jacob and Joseph will be a fire and a flame that will devour Esau as "stubble" and none of them shall remain. The final verses refer to the mount of Esau as being given over to those of the south and Jerusalem will possess the cities of the south but "saviors" shall come on mount Zion to judge the mount of Esau and "the kingdom shall be the Lord's." So this word is a rumor about the destruction of Edom because ultimately the Lord brings deliverance.

When Obadiah mentions the deception of those that are confederate with Edom in verse 7, we learn that they were at peace with them. I believe that this is a reference to the broken covenant in Daniel 11:23–24 when the Antichrist becomes strong and when he is in league with a small people as he comes in "peaceably" before he turns against them. It is the Lord that calls Esau/ Edom a small people in Obadiah 2. This occurs at the time of the abomination of desolation when those who know their God are tested and tried by sword, flame, captivity, and by spoil according to Daniel 11:31–36 as the Antichrist exalts himself above the Most High God. This coincides with Daniel 7:25 and Revelation 13:5–8 when the Antichrist wears out the saints by making war with them and is given power over them for forty-two months. Revelation 13:8 shows that only those whose names are not written in the "book of life of the Lamb" will worship the dragon and the beast. This beast in Revelation 13:1–5 that gets his life and is healed from a deadly wound by the dragon is said to be the one who speaks "great things and blasphemies" is identified in Daniel 7:25 as the fourth beast who speaks "great words against the Most High." This dragon requires all to receive the mark of 666 to buy or sell and to worship the image of the beast or be killed according to Revelation 13:16–18. This beast is the Antichrist. The dragon is Satan and does "great wonders, so that he makes fire come down from heaven on earth in the sight of men," according to verse Revelation 13:13. The interaction of these two figures explains Revelation 17:8 concerning the beast that "was and is not."

In Daniel 11:41, we read that the Antichrist enters the "glorious land" and overthrows many countries but "these will escape out of his hand, *even* Edom and Moab, and the chief of the children of Ammon. The God of Abraham, who promised the "glorious land" to his descendants, will keep His promise to the descendants of Isaac and Ishmael and Jacob and Esau whose names are in the Lamb's book of life by accepting Jesus as savior. They are the ones who will be alive to see the rise of the antichrist system and will not bow down to him or receive his mark.

Obadiah is one of several prophets that declare a redemptive provision for the descendants of Edom to be included in the kingdom of God despite their enmity toward Jacob also called Israel. Jeremiah 49:7–22 includes identical passages found in Obadiah about the grape gatherers leaving some grapes to glean, which represents a remnant, and the thieves which steal until they have enough (Compare Jeremiah 49:9 and Obadiah 5). Jeremiah 49:12 shows that Edom will not go unpunished. Jeremiah 49:14–16 reads the same as Obadiah 1–4 about the rumor from the Lord to rise up against Edom who the Lord is calling "small" and intends to "bring down" because of their pride. Jeremiah 49:22 states that the "heart of the mighty men of Edom" will be as the heart of a woman in her pangs." This is a reference to a woman in labor which is an analogy that Paul used in 1 Thessalonians 5:3 warning that when we hear talk of peace and safety then comes sudden destruction like a woman going into labor.

Jeremiah also writes in Lamentations 4:21–22 that even though the daughter of Edom will have to be punished, He will no longer make her suffer captivity. Ezekiel 25:12–14 declares that God will use Israel to perform His vengeance on Edom and 35:15 tells of the desolation the Lord will cause in Idumea, another term for Edom. Joel 3:19 also describes the desolation of Edom for the "violence against the children of Judah" when they "shed innocent blood in the land." Amos 9:11–12 lets us know that when the Lord builds up the temple as in the "days of old" that the house of David will possess the remnant of Edom and all the heathen that are called by the Lord's name. The true essence of the kinsmen redeemer rings through in this prophecy of Obadiah because the Lord does all that His righteous judgment requires yet is willing to "buy back" his inheritance even though Esau sold his birthright and didn't value his inheritance and traded it to meet his physical needs.

The Lord showed me how this prophecy also applies to Christians here and now. We are heirs with Christ. We are called the sons of God. We should treasure our standing in Christ and walk accordingly. Have we behaved in such a way that forsakes our birthright? To walk in His power and glory, we must recognize our standing in Christ. We are washed clean and set free as ministers of the Holy Word of God, Jesus. We must pray for the understanding that only the Holy Spirit can give to be able to instruct many as Daniel spoke of as we live in these last days that could see the rise of the antichrist system. We are our brother's keeper and need to reach out to all people with the good news of salvation through Jesus Christ and not ignore those who have forsaken their birthright as a child of God.

MICAH

MOUNTAINS MELTING LIKE WAX

Hear, all ye people; hearken, O earth, and all that therein is: and let the Lord God be witness against you, the Lord from his holy temple. For, behold, the Lord cometh forth out of his place, and will come down, and tread upon the high places of the earth. And the mountains shall be molten under him, and the valleys shall be cleft, as wax before the fire, *and* as the waters *that are* poured down a steep place. For the transgression of Jacob *is* all this, and for the sins of the house of Israel. What *is* the transgression of Jacob? is *it* not Samaria? and what *are* the high places of Judah? *are they* not Jerusalem? (Micah 1:2–5)

Micah was from a small town in Judah named Moresheth-gath and was a contemporary of Isaiah and Hosea having prophesied after them during the reigns of Jotham, Ahaz, and Hezekiah, the kings of Judah. Some of Micah's prophecies are similar to those of Isaiah as he spoke to warn the people of impending judgment for their sin of breaking the laws of Moses and for their worship of idols. He wrote during the time that the Jews lived in fear of the power of the Assyrians under Sennacherib. Second Kings 18:11–12 tells of Israel being taken captive to Assyria for their transgressions. However, 2 Kings 19:34–37 also shows how the Lord defended Zion for His own sake and for the sake of His servant David when he sent an angel to kill 185,000 in the Assyrians' camp which led Sennacherib to return to Nineveh where his sons killed him.

Micah's prophecies contain a two-fold truth for the people of his time as well as for the future when the Lord will come against all the nations who seek to destroy Jerusalem. Although the Lord allows the enemy to take His people by sword and captivity, ultimately the enemy will face the Lord's retribution.

Micah begins his prophecy in verse 2 with, "Hear, all ye people" and then includes all those on earth. So even though he specifically identifies Samaria as being the transgression of Jacob and the high places of Judah as being in Jerusalem in verse 5, he has a message for the world. In chapter 1 verses 3–4, Micah uses the imagery of the mountains melting, valleys being carved as wax could be by fire or like water coming down from a steep place when the Lord comes "out of his place to tread upon the high places of the earth." Zechariah 14:4 also tells of the time when the Lord stands on the mount of Olives and creates a great valley from east to west as the mount is severed. Revelation 6:14 describes the mountains and islands that "were moved out of their places" when the sixth seal is broken on the great day of the "wrath of the Lamb."

We previously considered the reality of the saints of the Most High being overcome by the antichrist. This is foretold in Daniel 7:25 when he "wears out the saints." In Daniel 11:33, when those that "understand" will fall by sword, flame, and captivity, and in Revelation 13:7, when the saints are "overcome" during that three-and-a-half-year period only to see their ultimate victory when Jesus comes to defeat him. Just as the angel of the Lord destroyed the 185,000 in the camp of the Assyrians; likewise, the Lord will come to destroy with the "sword of his mouth" all those in league with the false prophet and beast, who received the mark of the beast and came to make war with the Lord as He leads the armies of heaven according to Revelation 19:14; 19–21.

If Micah was speaking to all people of the earth and used the sins of Samaria and Jerusalem as an example, we too must be warned. The sins of Israel and Judah are explained in Micah 3:8–11.

> But truly I am full of power by the spirit of the Lord, and of judgment, and of might, to declare unto Jacob his transgression, and to Israel his sin. Hear this, I pray you, ye heads of the house of Jacob, and princes of the house of Israel, that abhor judgment, and pervert all equity. They build up Zion with blood, and Jerusalem with iniquity. The heads thereof judge for reward, and the priest thereof teach for hire and the prophets thereof divine for money: yet will they lean upon the Lord, and say, *Is* not the Lord among us? none evil can come upon us.

Is it any wonder that the church today is like that which is described in these verses? Even though I believe that there are ministries operating in the power of the Holy Spirit today, I am also aware of many ministries that are doing exactly what Micah described as the sins of Jacob and Israel. Jesus warned of all those that would come in His name but we are not to follow. How many current healing ministries ask for money to continue their work? How many "so-called prophets" write books full of "their own understanding" and sell them at churches and bookstores? How many evangelists are receiving the kind of praise that resembles idol worship? How many pastors have reverted to "feel good" messages to fill their churches? How many counselors in the church are using the psychology of the world? I think of the apostasy that will occur before Jesus comes back and fear for believers that fall prey to these false shepherds. Jesus warned about His sheep being scattered, but it is only with the wisdom and discernment of the Holy Spirit that we will hear the voice of the true Shepherd. The Holy Spirit will lead us in all truth as we search the word of God daily. Micah warned that the Lord would come to tread down the "high places" of the earth. He spoke directly to Samaria who was blatantly involved in idol worship when it was part of the northern kingdom and to Judah who followed their example in Jerusalem. It's as if Samaria represents the worldly influence that infects the true worship of the Holy One of Israel, who is a jealous God who told us not to have any other gods before Him. Individually, we can allow almost anything to become an idol if it interferes with our relationship with the Lord, and corporately, as a body of believers, we cannot allow the "high places" to be established in our midst.

HIRES BURNED WITH FIRE

Therefore I will make Samaria as an heap of the field, *and* as plantings of a vineyard: and I will pour down the stones thereof into the valley, and I will discover the foundations thereof. And all the graven images thereof shall be beaten to pieces, and all the hires thereof shall be burned with the fire and all the idols thereof will I lay desolate: for she gathered *it* of the hire of an harlot, and they shall return to the hire of an harlot. (Micah 1:6–7)

This is a continuation of the prophecy that Micah spoke to Samaria and the word hire is used to refer to those who benefited financially from the use of the graven images. Since these idols were made of wood and or precious metals, anyone involved in the construction and sale of these graven images, along with those in the temples who took the sacrifices made to these images, would be the ones that would be burned with fire. This practice of heathen worship is written about in 1 Kings 16:32 when Ahab, the son of Omri, built a temple and altar to Baal in Bethel. First Kings 18:19 makes a reference to the 450 prophets of Baal and the "four hundred prophets of the grove" who ate at Jezebel's table that Elijah invited to the challenge of his God versus their gods in calling down fire to consume their separate sacrifices. The God of Israel sent fire down to consume Elijah's sacrifice, but the prophets of Baal were unable to have their gods send fire down on their sacrifice and then Elijah killed them.

Isaiah, Jeremiah, Ezekiel, Hosea, and Amos joined Micah in declaring the judgment that Samaria would face for their idolatry and the severity of corrupt morals that followed as a result of their idol worship. This capital city of the ten tribes of Israel in the northern kingdom saw this judgment begin when it was attacked by the Assyrians and had its citizens taken captive and its population replaced with foreigners. History would show that Alexander the Great would do the same. Later, Herod the Great would rebuild and refortify the site and even though the apostle Phillip would succeed in spreading the gospel there, eventually the city on a hill in the center of Palestine would be reduced to ruins as prophesied by Micah.

The second part of this judgment found in Micah 1:7 tells that the idols will be laid desolate because Samaria hired herself as a harlot in the practice of idol worship and that she will "return to the hire of the harlot." Despite the idols being wiped out, this will not stop this practice of spiritual prostitution. While harlotry in essence meant adultery in the spiritual sense because other gods were replaced in the worship of the one true God of Israel, Micah makes it clear that this harlotry was done for the purpose of profit and that is why those that profit from idolatry will suffer the punishment of the fire of God. Notice in Revelation 18:3, it describes those merchants who became rich because of their involvement with the whore of Babylon. The whore of Babylon represents the "mystery religion" or global religion that will arise during the tribulation. These merchants will profit from this prostitution of religion and will see the demise of their commerce when, in one hour, the fire of God destroys Babylon according to Revelation 18:17–19. Ultimately, those involved with Babylon will be thrown into the lake of fire.

In Micah 1:9, it says that her "wound is incurable" and that it has come to Judah. The reference to "her" wound is changed to the pronoun "it" and then is referred to as "he" coming to the "gate" of God's people, "*even* to Jerusalem." I believe that the pronoun change is important. Consider that Samaria was once part of David's kingdom because "she" belonged to the Lord, and then she transferred her worship to idols, which became her wound. Once Judah followed Samaria's worship of graven images the wound refers to the worship of things and that is why the pronoun "it" is used. The wound takes on a masculine form as it comes to the "gate" of God's people, even to Jerusalem. The "gate" symbolizes the protection of the leadership, but in this case "his" wound has become incurable.

In chapter 2, we learn of the violence and oppression done against God's people because of the covetousness of those that "devise iniquity" and how the Lord will rescue His remnant like a flock of sheep in the midst of the fold. When Jesus described himself as the "gate," He used this image that was taken from the practice of the shepherd laying his body down at the entrance of the sheepfold to keep out anyone that would harm the flock. In His time, many different flocks were kept in one "sheepfold." In John 10:1–18, this analogy was used to warn against the "thief or robber" who entered the sheepfold by some other way and not by passing through the gate. That thief comes in to "kill, steal, and destroy." In this story of the good shepherd that lays down his life for his sheep, we also learn of the hireling that leaves the sheep when the wolf comes in to catch and scatter the sheep. Matthew 10:16 compares the apostles as being sent out as sheep among wolves. When Jesus told the story in the gospel of John, it says it was the Pharisees that did not understand what He was saying according to 10:6, and we know He was talking to the religious leaders according to 9:40. In John 10:4, Jesus says the true shepherd will go out before his sheep and the sheep will follow Him because they know His voice.

It was Micah that illustrated this in chapter 2 verse 13 when he told of the "breaker," a term used for the Messiah, that would pass through the gate to lead the sheep out as their "king before them" and as "the Lord as the head of them." It is the "hireling," the one that is paid to care for the flock that will not protect the sheep.

Micah's complaint found in the third chapter is against the "heads of Jacob," "the princes of the house of Israel," because they "hate the good and love the evil" in verses 1 and 2. They are the "hirelings" referred to in chapter 3 verse 11 as the "heads" that judge for reward, and the priests that teach for hire, and the prophets that "divine for money." Jesus was speaking to the Pharisees and if they had paid attention to Micah's prophecy, they would have known the Lord was revealing their sin to them and to His people.

The final verse of that chapter lets us know that Zion will be "plowed as a field" and Jerusalem will become "heaps" and the "mountain of the house as the high places of the forest." However, Micah 4:1 is a continuation of that word because it says,

> But in the last days it shall come to pass, *that* the mountains of the house of the Lord shall be established in the top of the mountains and it shall be exalted above the hills; and the people shall flow unto it.

So even though there will be destruction, there is a promise of a future kingdom. The following verses describe a time of peace when the Lord will teach, lead, judge, and speak as He gathers His remnant to enjoy the fruits of the land, which I believe refers to the millennium. Micah 4:8 says that the "first dominion" will come to the daughter of Zion and the kingdom shall come to the daughter of Jerusalem. Verses 9–13 revert back to Micah's day as he looks to the future of the daughter of Zion as she labors to bring forth and how the Lord will redeem her even when she is in Babylon. It is a time when Micah says many nations will come against her to "defile her," but the Lord will cause her to "thresh the nations."

Micah prophesied of the coming Messiah in a verse used in Christmas cards that says the ruler of Israel would come out of Bethlehem in chapter 5 verse 2, but looks to the deliverance of the remnant in the future that will be in the midst of many people as the Lord destroys the land of the Assyrians and the land of Nimrod which is Babylon in verses 4 to 8. The Lord's "vengeance in anger" is to cease the idol worship in the remaining verses of chapter 5.

Chapter 6 contains one of the most well-used verses from Micah, a response to the question of what is good and what does the Lord require, verse 8 says that the Lord showed him, "to do justly and to love mercy, and to walk humbly with thy God." This comes in the context of the Lord's controversy with His people in verse 2 as he pleads for Israel.

The final chapter once again is a reminder to the religious leaders of Micah's day that there are "none upright among men" according to verse 2. Micah feels the weight of the judgment to come as he cries out "Woe is me" in the first verse and declares, "I will bear the indignation of the Lord, because I have sinned against him, until he plead my cause and execute judgment for me: he will bring me forth to the light, *and* I shall behold his righteousness" in verse 9.

Despite the desolation according to verse 13 and the fear of the Lord in verse 17, the words of Micah end with hope in verses 18–20:

Who *is* a God like unto thee, that pardoneth iniquity, and passeth by the transgression of the remnant of his heritage? he retaineth not his anger for ever, because he delighteth *in* mercy. He will turn again, he will have compassion upon us; he will subdue our iniquities; and thou wilt cast all their sins into the depth of the sea. Thou wilt perform the truth to Jacob, *and* the mercy to Abraham, which thou hast sworn unto our fathers from the days of old.

What the Lord requires of all is what the Lord will do for all. He humbly became our good shepherd. He mercifully forgives and forgets our sins. He will come back to righteously judge the living and the dead.

6

NAHUM

Who can stand before his indignation? and who can abide
in the fierceness of his anger? his fury is poured like fire,
and the rocks are thrown down by him. (Nahum 1:6)

Nahum was from a village in Palestine called Elkosh and
prophesied to Judah and not the ten tribes; however, this book
begins with the phrase "The burden of Nineveh." It is a warning
that God will overthrow the world power that oppresses God's
kingdom. Nineveh was the capital of the Assyrian Empire that
held the people of Judah captive after many invasions. Nineveh
was built by the Babylonians according to Genesis 10:10–11.
These verses indicate that Asshur, a descendant of Nimrod, went
out from Babylon to build Nineveh. The word Assyria is a Greek
derivation of the name Asshur. Nimrod was a descendent of Shem
according to Genesis 10:22 and is best known for attempting to

build a tower to heaven in the land of Shinar, which became the Tower of Babel, where God prevented them and confused their languages according to Genesis 11:1–9.

So although the people of Nineveh worshipped their guardian goddess Ishtar as a result of the Babylonian influence, they were a Semitic people. The Babylonian influence on Palestine was seen as early as the sixteenth century BC because the officials in Palestine used Babylonian script and language in their communications with the Egyptian court. A king of Babylon developed a system of social laws named after him as the Code of Hammurabi around 1700 BC.

In 1270 BC, Babylonia came under the control of the Assyrians. It wasn't until 625 BC that Babylonia became independent as a result of an alliance by an Assyrian official named Nabopolassar with the Chaldeans (another name for Babylonians). His reign lasted until 605 BC. The preceding year, Nineveh was captured and destroyed. Then the land west of the Euphrates including Palestine was partitioned which led to the monarchy of Nebuchadnezzar. Despite Egypt's claim to this land, Pharaoh Necho was defeated by Nebuchadnezzar at the famous battle of Carchemish in 605 BC. This led to a forty-four-year reign that helped Babylon reach its greatest limits. History shows these two dominions as being simultaneous with either Babylon or Nineveh in authority. Given the most ancient history of Genesis and realizing that one evolved from the other, I believe that they can be referred to as synonymous in prophetic language.

In Jonah 1:2 and 3:3, Nineveh is referred to as the "great city," which included Rehoboth-Ir, Calah, and Resen according to Genesis 10:11–12. Notice that Revelation 17:18 calls the woman, who John saw riding the red beast, "the great city which reigneth over the kings of the earth." Nahum 3:1 calls Nineveh the "bloody city" because of violence done to the surrounding nations by the Assyrian Empire. It was the practice of one of their kings, Ashurnasirpal, to dismember their captives and then behead them to build a mound of human heads. Nahum 3:3 describes the great number of corpses that have fallen in the bloody city. In the following verse, Nahum begins to describe this city as the "wellfavoured harlot, the mistress of witchcrafts, that selleth nations through her whoredoms, and families through her witchcrafts." All of Revelation 18 describes the way this great city became rich as a result of her prostituting herself with the nations of the world through commerce and how she will be destroyed by fire when God comes to judge her.

Nahum 1:11 tells of a wicked counselor that will come out of Nineveh that imagines evil against the Lord. In verses 1–5 of the first chapter, it says,

> God *is* jealous, and the Lord revengeth; the Lord revengeth, and *is* furious; the Lord will take vengeance on his adversaries and he reserveth *wrath* for his enemies. The Lord is slow to anger and great in power and will not at all *acquit the wicked*: the Lord *hath* his way in the whirlwind and in the storm, and the clouds are the dust of his feet. He rebuketh the sea, and maketh it dry, and drieth up all the rivers: Bashan languisheth, and Carmel and the flower of Lebanon languisheth. The mountains quake at him and the hills melt, and the earth is burned at his presence, yea, the world, and all that dwell therein.

Nahum mentions three areas that languish. To languish means to restlessly long or pine for something. Carmel and Lebanon are in the midst of mountains and Bashan is in on open land but all are in the northern kingdom of Israel. So why is Judah's prophet telling them about Nineveh and Israel?

When he speaks of God's fire, he says that the mountains quake, the hills melt, and the whole world is burned. So his message is to the ancient land of Assyria, to the land of his time, and to all the lands of the world. When Jonah was told to prophesy to Nineveh, he refused at first because of its reputation for wickedness. Even after the city repented at his word, Jonah was mad at God for not destroying them. In Jonah 4:4, God asks Jonah if he "does well to be angry?" but he didn't reply. When God destroys the gourd that gave him shade on the hilltop east of Nineveh, he asked Jonah again "if he does well to be angry?" with God for destroying the plant. Jonah replied in 4:9 that he was right to be angry even to the point of death. In the following verses, God reprimands him for caring more about a plant than the 120,000 people in Nineveh. God explains that these people "cannot discern between their right hand and their left hand." In Jonah 3, when he speaks to the people of Nineveh, he only tells them that God will destroy the city in forty days. Their king tells everyone to fast and stop their evil ways. I get the impression that until Jonah and the king had spoken that no one in the city had ever been warned about their behavior.

We are living in a society that has tried to eliminate God from the public's awareness. There is a generation that has grown up, many of whom have never learned anything about Jesus. Many people have never heard about God's judgment except through a secular point of view, which is a perversion and mockery of the truth. They have no knowledge of the purpose of the death of Christ to pay for their sin debt. And unless that message is delivered with the unconditional love of God, they will never understand.

At the same time, it seems to me that many churches have forgotten the fear of the Lord. The churches that are too obsessed with how their congregation feels and only share the inviting pleasant words in the Bible are guilty of sharing half-truths and misrepresent God's fury and indignation at the wickedness in the world. Revelation talks of a fourth of the earth being burned up. Nahum says the wicked will be burned as stubble in chapter 1 verse 10.

How many leaders of Christian ministries are guilty of buying a cruise ticket like Jonah instead of sharing the warnings of the prophets? If the people are not warned, then those church leaders will have blood on their hands. We could look at many cities in America that could resemble a modern day Nineveh and I know that there are ministries that are reaching out to them. We could look at some neighborhoods in much the same way. We could also know individuals who are like the Ninevites of Jonah's day. We could look from across the ocean at the Middle East and have a Jonah-like attitude for those who don't understand the message of Jesus, or we can pray and ask God how he could use believers to help them.

In regard to end-time events, Nahum 1:9 declares that God will make an "utter end" of Nineveh. The remains of the ancient city have been discovered so that prophecy awaits fulfillment. I believe the antichrist system will include the Assyrian–Babylonian empire and might help explain Revelation 17:10–11when John talks about the eighth king that is of the seven kingdoms. However, it is the "stone that was cut without hands" that is spoken of in Daniel 2:34 that destroys the "image of different metals" referring to the powers that be in the end times. It is the entire image that collapses when the stone breaks the feet made of clay and iron. That stone represents Jesus, the stone that was rejected. Nahum 1:7 reads, "The Lord *is* good, a strong hold in the day of trouble; and he knoweth them that trust in him." This is the way Jesus needs to be represented to those who have no understanding of His love.

THE FIRE WILL DEVOUR

Behold, thy people in the midst of thee *are* women: the gates of thy land shall be set wide open unto thine enemies: the fire shall devour thy bars. Draw thee waters for the siege, fortify thy strong holds: go into clay, and tread the mortar, make strong the brickkiln. There shall the fire devour thee; the sword shall cut thee off, it shall eat thee up like the cankerworm: make thyself many as the cankerworm, make thyself many as the locust. (Nahum 3:13–15)

Nahum is warning Nineveh of its judgment, but within the first chapter, he describes how the earth and all that live on it are burned at the presence of the Lord in verse 5. The apostle Peter speaks of the elements burning with intense heat at the presence of the Lord. Verse 8 of Nahum 1 speaks of an "overrunning flood" that the Lord will use to bring an "utter end to the place thereof." The following verse again uses the phrase "utter end" to describe what the Lord will do. Then he speaks of a wicked counselor that will come out of Nineveh to "imagine evil against the Lord." Verse 14 explains that the Lord will make a grave out of their temples because they are "vile."

Next is a strange interlude before a continuation of the predicated doom. Nahum encourages Judah to keep their "solemn feasts and perform their vows" because the wicked will no longer go through their land because they are "utterly cut off." This is one of only two references made to the Hebrews in the entire book of Nahum. One is the fifteenth verse of the first chapter directed to Judah and is a more familiar verse which begins with, "Behold upon the mountains the feet of him that bringeth good tidings, that publisheth peace!" The other is found in chapter 2 verse 2 where we are told, "the Lord has turned away the excellency of Jacob and the excellency of Israel" because "the emptiers have emptied them out and marred their vine branches." The inclusion of these references to Nahum's people comes almost as if he is trying to catch his breath in the midst of all the violence he has viewed in this prophetic vision.

The destruction that is to come upon Nineveh is further described in chapters 2 and 3. In chapter 2 verse 7, Huzzab, a poetic term is used for Nineveh. It means "queen" according to an ancient version of the Old Testament called the Targums. The Targums were writings that were based on the verbal translations necessary for the Hebrews that began speaking Aramaic, mistakenly called Chaldee, after Babylonian captivity. I see this as a reference to the same queen in Revelation 18:7–8 where we read of the fallen Babylon:

> How much she hath glorified herself, and lived deliciously, so much torment and sorrow give her: for she saith in her heart, I sit a queen and am no widow, and shall see no sorrow. Therefore shall her plagues come in one day, death, and mourning and famine; and she shall be utterly burned with fire, for strong is the Lord God who judgeth her.

The remainder of the second chapter of Nahum continues with scenes of flaming devastation.

Chapter 3 describes the iniquity of this queen who is also described as the "well-favored harlot" until we read in verse 7 that she is laid waste because the Lord is against her. In verse 8, Nahum is comparing Nineveh to No, which is No Amon, also known as Thebes, an ancient city in Egypt. The word Amon refers to their main deity. It was the capital and center of the flourishing Egyptian civilization until Esarhaddon, the king of Assyria, conquered it in 672 BC. This king's son, Ashurbanipal, later took control over the country and destroyed the city in 664 BC. Today, this area is best known for its temples, obelisks, and sphinxes at Luxor and Karnak on both sides of the Nile River. This verse indicates that the waters were all around No and that the rampart and wall were the sea. Nahum goes on to say in the next verse that "Ethiopia and Egypt were her strength, and *it was* infinite; Put and Lubim were thy helpers." Put and Lubim are generally considered to be African people related to the Egyptians. Even though ancient Egypt was overcome by Assyria, the Lord completely overcomes Assyria with a fire that will annihilate any remembrance of her. When Nahum writes in 3:15 that Nineveh will be eaten up and if by a cankerworm, he's trying to portray the image of their demise. In verse 17, he shows how their kings and warriors will disappear even as locusts and grasshoppers do when the heat of day comes.

It is this Assyrian dynasty, encompassing Nineveh/Babylon that is part of the major kingdoms represented in the image that Daniel interpreted for the king of Babylon in Chapter 2. In verse 35, after the stone breaks down the image we read, then was the iron, the clay, the brass, the silver, and the gold, broken to pieces together. Daniel told the king of Babylon that he was the head of gold; Babylon was later incorporated into the Assyrian Kingdom. This clarifies Revelation 17:10 which speaks of seven kings, of which five have fallen and one is yet to come. The beast, who creates the image to be worshipped in Revelation 13, is the one who was and is not, and is the eighth and of the seven, of Revelation 17:11.

While much focus for the fulfillment of end-time prophecies looks to the revived Roman Empire which is represented by the legs and feet of Daniel's image, I emphasize the need to focus on the other kingdoms as well, the arms of silver representing Persia and the belly of brass representing Greece. It is the entire image that is broken down. While some consider the revived Roman Empire to be connected with Rome, Italy, at the time that Constantine established Christianity as the state religion in the third century, Constantinople became known as the "New Rome," thus creating a dual rulership which explains the image having two legs. This region is modern day Istanbul in Turkey. Babylon is in Iraq and Persia is modern day Iran. So it is imperative to watch the interaction of these world powers today as we are led closer to the time when the Lord will intervene in the affairs of men. Daniel 2:42–43 explains that the toes of this image are part clay and part iron signifying weakness and strength and it is because "they will mingle themselves with the seed of men: but they shall not cleave one to another, even as iron is not mixed with clay." The kingdoms of men will give their power to the beast that receives his power from the dragon, which is Satan.

In the final verses of Nahum, the king of Assyria is told that "Thy shepherds slumber" and all "thy nobles shall dwell *in the dust*: thy people is scattered upon the mountains *and* no man gathereth *them*." Nahum completes his vision by saying that everyone will clap their hands when they hear of the devastation because no one escaped being effected by "their wickedness."

Nahum's vision of the "burden of Nineveh" was spoken to Judah because they needed to know the lack of power of those who oppose God when he prophesied the destruction of their enemies. This word would give hope for the deliverance of their people. It is the same for us today as it was in Nahum's time and because we know these truths, we are to continue "steadfast and undismayed" in our service and worship to the Most High God.

HABAKKUK

LABOR IN THE FIRE

Behold, *is it* not of the Lord of hosts that the people shall labour in the very fire, and the people shall weary themselves for very vanity? (Habakkuk 2:13)

Habakkuk is a word that means "embrace" or possibly "a garden plant" and is the name of a prophet of Judah who belonged to the tribe of Levi. The third chapter is not only a prayer but also a song because in the last verse it says what he wrote is for "the chief singer on my stringed instruments." The phrase "upon Shigionoth" found in chapter 3 verse 1 is a musical term and is also found in Psalm 7 and means to use an erratic, wild, or enthusiastic rhythm while singing those words. So Habakkuk was also involved in temple worship as a writer and musician besides being a prophet of God. Within this eighth book of the Minor Prophets are found three complaints to God and His responses to a list of five woes as judgment for five types of wickedness and a prayer of praise invoking and petitioning God to use mercy while administering His wrath.

The first complaint is spoken as if God is not hearing Habakkuk's cry against the violence and wickedness he sees in his land in chapter 1 verses 2–4. The Lord responds in verses 5–6 by warning Judah that he will use the Chaldeans to punish the guilty. The second complaint comes as a result of the first when Habakkuk cannot understand why God would allow those that are more righteous to be destroyed by the wicked Chaldeans. The reason is found in chapter 2 verse 4 as part of a familiar verse which says, "The just shall live by faith." However, the intent of the Lord's response is that all the unrighteous and prideful are doomed.

In the tenth chapter of Isaiah, it explains how even though the Lord will use the Assyrians as the "rod of his anger" in verse 5, when the Lord has finished His work on Mt. Zion, He will "punish the fruit of the stout heart of the king of Assyria, and the glory of his high looks" as found in Isaiah 5:12. Verses 13–18 tell us that because this King thinks that he has been victorious because of his own power, the Lord will prove to him that he is the One that is wielding the strength by devouring him and his glory with fire. The Lord speaks through Isaiah when He compares the king of Assyria to an axe that takes the credit for chopping wood in verse 15. (See verse studies from Isaiah 9 and 10 in *Fire in the Bible: Genesis-Daniel* for background information on Assyrians/Chaldeans).

As far as Habakkuk is concerned, his worries are alleviated because he understands the basic truth that "the just shall live by faith" and consequently is able to declare the judgments against this great world power in the second part of this prophecy. He is also able to worship God's might and majesty and give Him praise despite desperate conditions because of the quiet confidence of his faith.

Although the writings of Habakkuk are not dated, we know that the temple was still standing because chapter 2 verse 20 mentions that "the Lord *is* in his holy temple: let all the earth keep silence before him" and because the book ends with the words that show us musical services were still being conducted when Habakkuk writes directions for how the music is to be played. The first chapter describes the conquering reputation of the Chaldeans and places the time frame as they were beginning to subdue other nations. Habakkuk writes in chapter 1 verse 7 that they are "terrible and dreadful" and in verse 8 we see part of "the burden" which this prophet saw. He writes, "Their horses also are swifter than the leopards, and are more fierce than the evening wolves: and their horsemen shall spread themselves, and their horsemen shall come from far; they shall fly as the eagle *that* hasteth to eat." Their violently cruel methods of warfare were well known by all nations and are the just provocation for their destruction. The Chaldeans, who revolted from the Assyrians in 625 BC, continued to dominate and subjugate other nations and attained leadership among the world powers when they overcame Nineveh in 607 BC and were victorious against the Egyptians at Carchemish in 605 BC. In chapter 2, we read in the beginning verses that Habakkuk says,

> I will stand upon my watch, and set me upon the tower and will watch to see what he will say unto me, and what I shall answer when I am reproved. And the Lord answered me, and said, Write the vision, and make *it* plain upon tables, that he may run that readeth it. For the vision *is* yet for the appointed time, but at the end it shall speak, and not lie: though it tarry, wait for it; because it will surely come, it will not tarry.

Oftentimes, this verse is quoted out of context and used to refer to those things that an individual believes God to accomplish in their lives. In Proverbs 29:18, we read that "with no vision," God's people will perish. In 1 Samuel 3:1, we read that "the word of the Lord was precious in those days; *there was* no open vision." Imagine if you were Habakkuk and had to reveal to the wicked people of his generation that they would be attacked and become subject to a vicious nation. The destruction of Judah would happen because God would use the Chaldeans to punish His own people. No wonder Habakkuk calls this vision a burden.

Isaiah 10:24–25 and Micah 4:11–14 give insight and comfort. Isaiah writes,

> Therefore thus saith the Lord God of hosts, O my people that dwellest in Zion, be not afraid of the Assyrian: he shall smite thee with a rod, and shall lift up his staff against thee, after the manner of Egypt. For yet a very little while, and the indignations shall cease, and mine anger in their destruction. Micah wrote: Now also many nations are gathered against thee, that say, Let her be defiled, and let our eye look upon Zion. But they know not the thoughts of the Lord, neither understand they his counsel: for he shall gather them as the sheaves into the floor. Arise and thresh, O daughter of Zion: for I will make thine horn iron, and I will make thy hoofs brass: and thou shalt beat in pieces many people: and I will consecrate their gain unto the Lord and their substance unto the Lord of the whole earth.

While I have seen footnotes and cross-references that write of these prophecies as having been fulfilled. I caution every serious Bible student to carefully consider the information. The understanding of "near and far fulfillment" is a critical way of studying prophecy. The Chaldeans did overcome Judah and the people were taken into captivity. Who are the people that labor in the fire and wear themselves out for vain reason? Why is it that the Lord would have it be this way? The work that the Hebrew captives performed was to benefit the Chaldeans and it served the vain desires of the Assyrian's/Chaldean's kingdom. Yes, God allowed it in previous history and I believe that He will allow the saints of the Most High to be overcome for a season during the times of the antichrist in the future. Daniel and Revelation write of these challenges for God's people. It is under the captivity of the antichrist system that the four kingdoms rise to power that will subdue all other nations for the purpose of forming a one world government, religion, and economic system.

Habakkuk speaks a warning to God's people today. We cannot allow the body of Christ to become captive to a culture of violence and greed, unless we wish to see our enemies have dominion over us being used to inflict God's punishment. Although His love is unconditional, His benefits come with conditions. If you obey Him, you will know His blessings. If you disobey Him, you will know His judgments. The Lord desires obedience rather than sacrifice. Even more critical is the fact that the Lord knows we love Him when we obey Him.

This speaks to us individually as well. If we think of staying "on fire" for the Lord, that means that we have to stay disciplined in our search of the scriptures and in our time spent in prayer and meditation. It is in the vain things that we will grow weary. Let us be filled with the knowledge of His glory from the time we spend in His presence loving Him.

8

ZEPHANIAH

Neither their silver nor their gold shall be able to deliver them in the day of the Lord's wrath; but the whole land shall be devoured by the fire of his jealousy: for he shall make even a speedy riddance of all them that dwell in the land…Therefore wait ye upon me, saith the Lord, until the day that I rise up to the prey: for my determination is to gather the nations, that I may assemble the kingdoms, to pour upon them mine indignation *even* all my fierce anger: for all the earth shall be devoured with the fire of my jealousy. (Zephaniah 1:18; 3:8)

The meaning of Zephaniah's name is a comfort to the one who brought a powerful message of judgment to his people and to the people of all nations for their wickedness and idolatry. It means "Jehovah has hidden." Zephaniah's ancestry was traced back to King Hezekiah and he lived and worked during Josiah's reign according to the first verse of this book. This timing is confirmed in chapter 2 verse 4 because Gath is not named as one of the Philistine cities and because Nineveh still existed at that time and there is also no mention of the Chaldeans.

The doctrine of God's universal judgment is the essence of this prophetic book. In the first chapter, we read of the all-consuming destruction and the overthrowing of all idolatry. Sinners in Judah will receive their judgment and the day of wrath will come because of rampant wickedness. The second chapter explains that the only means of escape is through repentance. Zephaniah's message is a call for all those who fear God to be humble and seek Jehovah in the hope of being delivered. Chapter 3 is a guarantee that God will punish other nations for their evil and foresees that Jerusalem will not escape because they don't repent even though the Lord is in their midst. The blessings that come as a result of this judgment will be that the nations turn to the Lord and the remnant will trust in Him and be holy. Also, the Lord will reign in glory and be a blessing to His people, gathered from their captivity, to be praise in all the earth.

Zephaniah 1:2–3 reads,

> I will utterly consume all *things* from off the land, saith Lord. I will consume man and beast; I will consume the fowls of the heaven and the fishes of the sea, and the stumblingblocks with the wicked, and I will cut off man from off the land, saith Lord.

In the following verses, we read that the Lord will "stretch out his hand" against Judah and Jerusalem and "cut off the remnant of Baal from this place *and* the name of the Chemarims with the priest; And them that worship the host of heaven upon the housetops; and them that worship *and* swear by the Lord, and that swear by Malcham; And them that are turned back from the Lord; and *those* that have not sought the Lord, nor inquired for him."

The Chemarims were the priest of the high places, the calves at Bethel and of Baal. Second Kings 23:5 tells how King Josiah got rid of these priests who worshipped the sun, moon, planets, and hosts of heaven, who had burned incense to these pagan deities that today make up the signs of the zodiac in astrology. Hosea 10:5 tells how the priests and the people of Samaria will mourn when the glory of the temple is gone because they worshipped the sacred cows in Bethel at the time when ten of the tribes of Israel formed the northern kingdom and used that temple in place of the one in Jerusalem.

Zephaniah's complaint from the Lord is that these people, who worshipped these pagan deities and golden calves, were from the tribes of Israel who knew they should worship the one, true God, Jehovah, and no other gods. neither have they "sought the Lord nor inquired for him." They are the ones who have turned away from God and have stopped seeking Him. Zephaniah is warning the people of Maktesh because of the impending doom. The word means: a mortar, a trough, a hollow. The Targum says it's the Kidron Valley but it is also considered the valley that separates the temple from the city. The Lord is speaking in this prophecy that He will gather the nations together in chapter 3 verse 8 to do what He has determined and that is to "rise up to the prey" to punish the whole earth with the fire of his jealousy. Revelation 16:16 calls this place of gathering Armageddon, a word formed from the name of a town called Megiddo. This site was well known as a battlefield where Israel's oppressors, the Canaanites, were defeated, and where Ahaziah, king of Judah, and King Josiah were killed in separate wars. It is believed that John used this term to help God's people identify this gathering place with this battleground of sorrow and triumph.

Zechariah also speaks of when the Lord will gather all nations together against Jerusalem in chapter14. It says that at that time, the Lord will stand on the Mount of Olives and a valley will be created when the great earthquake occurs. At that time, the saints will come with the Lord. Whether it is the Kidron Valley or an area of land that separates the temple from the city...the imagery is obvious. These are the people that are involved with the merchants, those that go about their business believing that the Lord will neither do good or evil according to Zephaniah 1:12. Notice that in the verses we are studying, it says that neither silver nor gold will deliver them in the day of the Lord's wrath.

Luke 21:20 records the Lord telling his disciples to know that the time of desolation is close when they see the nations gather for war around Jerusalem. In the second chapter of Zephaniah, we read of many different locations and if you take time to look at an ancient map, these are all neighboring regions surrounding Israel. Gaza, Ashkelon, Ashdod, and Ekron are along the coast to the southwest of Jerusalem. The Cherethites, supposedly Canaanites, descended from those who emigrated from Crete, along with the inhabitants of Canaan and the land of the Philistine are west of Jerusalem along the shore of the Mediterranean. I find it fascinating that the threat of modern day Palestinian extremists is to "push Israel into the sea" thereby granting them that coastal region. As of February 18, 2005, the surrender of the Gaza Strip was one of the conditions to be met in order to further the Middle East peace process as a precursor to the creation of a Palestinian state.

Zephaniah 2:8 also tells us because of the "reproach of Moab" and the "revilings of the children of Ammon" against "my people" because they have "magnified themselves against their border." the Lord will make Moab like Sodom and Ammon like Gomorrah and turn it into a perpetual desolation. Moab and Ammon are the regions to the east of the Dead Sea. Consider the dispute over these borders since Israel became a nation in 1948 and fought for their rights to the Temple Mount in 1967. Other regions listed in this chapter are Assyria to the north along with Nineveh and completing the circle is Ethiopia to the south on the other side of the Persian Gulf. In chapter 2, Zephaniah begins by telling the people to:

Gather yourselves together, yea, gather together, O nation not desired; Before the decree bring forth, *before* the day pass as the chaff before the fierce anger of the Lord come upon you before the day of the Lord's anger come upon you.

While chapter 2 speaks of destruction, chapter 3 is about the mercy God will have for His remnant. Zephaniah describes the filthy, polluted, and oppressing city in verse 1. In verse 2, he writes, "She obeyed not the voice; she received not correction, she trusted not in the Lord; she drew not near to her God." He goes on to tell of the corruption among the princes and judges who devour the people like wolves and lions. The prophets of Jerusalem are called "light *and* treacherous persons" and the priest have "polluted the sanctuary" and we learn that they have done "violence to the law." Even though the Lord is faithful to them, we realize as Zephaniah completes his description of the state of affairs in Jerusalem in verse 5, that "the unjust knoweth no shame." His remnant lives under these conditions so it is no wonder that He returns for them with the fire of His jealousy.

In verse 9, we learn that the Lord will "turn to the people a pure language that they may all call upon the Lord, to serve him with one consent." These people will not sin or speak lies; neither will they be afraid anymore according to verse 13. The phrase "turn to the people a pure language" is intriguing because it could be taken two ways and either way I believe is correct. One way would be to say the Lord would give them a pure language or the other way He would return to a people that spoke purely. I have also heard it said that this referred to people that speak in tongues. It is the Holy Spirit that gives us "utterance" as we pray to God in a spiritual language. I believe that all who have the Holy Spirit should be able to speak in tongues but when and how that happens is not for me to decide because the Bible teaches that the Holy Spirit "moves according as He wills."

I have been in fellowships where the attitude is one in which people are prayed for to receive that gift as if they are demanding it to be given. I speak for myself when I say it's no longer a gift if it's demanded. When I speak in tongues, I have often thought it might be an ancient language because when the apostles spoke tongues in public, there were people of many nations present who understood them. I understand what I am saying if the Lord reveals it to me, but that doesn't always happen. In chapter 3 verse 9, we also learn the people serve the Lord "with one consent." In other words, they are in unity. When Solomon's temple was dedicated, the people were as one when they worshipped; consequently, the glory of the Lord was manifested.

The most beautiful promise of the Lord through Zephaniah is found in chapter 3 verses 16–17: "In that day, it shall be said to Jerusalem, Fear thou not: *and to* Zion, Let not thine hands be slack. The Lord thy God in the midst of thee *is* mighty; he will save, he will rejoice over thee with joy; he will rest in his love, he will joy over thee will singing." Take the time to slowly consider these verses and imagine what it would be like to hear the Lord singing over His people with great joy as He rest in His love for them. Imagine what it was like for all those in the Bible who heard God speak. The Bible is compiled from ancient texts miraculously preserved and translated from the language of the Hebrews and Greeks, and we can hear the voice of God known as Jehovah-Jah-Eloihim-Adonay-Yahweh speaks through its pages.

9

ZECHARIAH

A WALL OF FIRE

For I, saith the Lord, will be unto her a wall of fire round about, and will be the glory in the midst of her. (Zechariah 2:5)

Zechariah is listed as the eleventh minor prophet who lived between 520 and 479 BC. His first recorded prophecy came during the second year of Darius Hystaspis, whose rule began in 520 BC. Haggai, Zerubbabel, and Joshua, the high priest were his contemporaries. Zechariah shared in proclaiming the message of these men by calling for a resumption of the building of the house of God. It is most probable that Zechariah was born in Babylon while the nation of Israel was held captive there. He is called a young man by the angel in his vision and began to prophesy when he was eighteen years old. The exiles returned to Jerusalem in 538 BC and had been there for more than eighteen years when Zechariah began to speak the word of the Lord. Zechariah belonged to the tribe of Levi. He was a priest just as Jeremiah and Ezekiel were and he was aware of the priest's responsibilities. Zechariah assumed the role of a priest because his grandfather named Iddo was the head of the priestly house of Joiakim, the son of Jeshua. It is believed that Zechariah's father, Berechiah, had died early, which placed Zechariah in this position at a young age.

There are eight visions that form the foundation of the whole book of Zechariah. Verse 3 of chapter 1 is the theme of this prophetic work. It reads, "Therefore say thou unto them, Thus saith the Lord of hosts; Turn ye unto me, saith the Lord of hosts, and I will turn unto you saith the Lord of hosts." In essence, the Lord is trying to get his people to learn the lessons of the past from the mistakes of their fathers, whom the Lord was very displeased with. Even though the Lord had sent His prophets to tell the people to turn from their evil ways, they would not, so they deserved the punishment of captivity. Now that they were back in their own land, the Lord is trying to draw them back to Himself through the words of Zechariah.

Verse 5 in chapter 2 is a promise of restoration of God's presence among His people. The eight visions, which begin this prophetic work, are a central theme to the whole book accredited to Zechariah. The first vision introduces the remaining seven and begins by telling us that Zechariah sees this vision at night. This vision comes three months after Zechariah received the word of the Lord found in the first six verses of chapter 1 demonstrating how the prophet waited on the Lord.

When Zechariah sees this vision, starting in verse 7, of red, white, and speckled horses, it appears to me that he is asking the one who rode the red horse for an explanation. He calls this man, "my Lord" but He is also referred to as the angel of the Lord. The horses have traveled all over the earth and reported back to the Lord that the earth is at rest. However, we learn the Lord is extremely displeased with the heathen and is jealous for his people Israel and intends to punish their oppressors.

I believe verse 12 is a discourse between the Father and the Son because it reads as follows "Then the angel of the Lord answered and said, O Lord of hosts, how long wilt thou not have mercy on Jerusalem and on the cities of Judah, against which thou hast had indignation these threescore and ten years?" The seventy years of desolation are the years of captivity that Jeremiah spoke of and also are referred to in Daniel 9:2. There is also the seventy weeks of years used as a timeline of events for the accomplishment of end-time prophecies, taken from the book of Daniel, of which we are awaiting the fulfillment of the final week to usher in the millennial reign of Jesus on earth. (See the segment called Furious Fire, in my first book, *Fire in the Bible: Genesis-Daniel*, regarding Jeremiah 21:8–14.)

The return of the Jews to Jerusalem from Babylonian captivity essentially marked the end of a seventy-year period. However, I believe that there is understanding to be gained from studying the history of that segment of time that ushered in the rebuilding of Zerubbabel's temple, and how it relates to the end-time events that will bring about the building of another temple and the desolations that the Lord intends to accomplish before He will return to rule and reign in Jerusalem during the millennium.

In Zechariah 1:13, we learn that the angel of the Lord speaks "good words and comfortable words" to Zechariah before we hear the Lord's complaint of verse 15. I have to wonder what those good words of comfort were. In the next two verses, we learn that the Lord will return to Jerusalem so that His house can be built in it and that prosperity will also come to His cities that will be spread abroad. I believe that this is not only a vision of the times we are living in because we know that the Word tells us that the Lord inhabits the praises of His people, but also points to the time when the Lord will rule from Jerusalem.

The Word of the Lord is timeless and is applicable not only to the time of Zechariah, but to our time as well and to the time when He will return. What follows are two more visions which lead up to the verse about the Lord being a "wall of fire" around Jerusalem. These verses explain that there are "four horns," representing rulerships that have scattered Judah, Israel, and Jerusalem. It is one thing to understand the dispersion of the Jewish nation all over the world, but we also need to recognize the move of God that will return the remnant of His people back to Israel before He returns.

The continuation of this vision is of four carpenters and when Zechariah asks what they have come to do, the Lord answers in verse 21 "These *are* the horns which have scattered Judah, so that no man did lift up his head: but these are come to fray (frighten) them to cast out the horns of the Gentiles, which lifted up *their* horn over the land of Judah to scatter it." Notice it is the four carpenters that are the horns that only scattered Judah and their intent is to fight against the powers of the Gentiles that also were involved in the dispersion of those in Judah only.

It is also necessary to realize that in the above verse, the four horns become one horn. Through careful examination and cross referencing of Daniel 7:1–8 and Revelation 17:10–13, there is an understanding to be gained by recognizing the interaction of the four horns in Daniel and how the ten kings in Revelation essentially will be four that give their power to the fourth kingdom. The fourth beast in Daniel actually has ten horns that are represented by four beasts. The fourth beast is also called a horn and is the one that "plucks up the first three horns." In both Revelation 13 and Daniel 7, the visions seen come up out of the sea. In both books, it is the fourth and final kingdom or horn that the enemy establishes that speaks abominable words against the Most High God.

Daniel 7:23–24 is an explanation given by one who stood by Daniel during his vision of the Ancient of Days. It reads,

Thus he said, the fourth beast shall be the fourth kingdom upon the earth, which shall be diverse from all kingdoms, and shall devour the whole earth, and shall tread it down, and break it in pieces. And the ten horns out of this kingdom are ten kings *that* shall arise: and another shall rise after them; and he shall be diverse from the first, and he shall subdue three kings.

The dominion of the fourth ruler will seek to wear out the saints of the Most High God just as Revelation 13:7 reveals that during this time that the saints are overcome only because that power was given to this fourth beast. However, we are told in the tenth verse, "Here is the patience and faith of the saints." Ultimately, we learn from Daniel in 7:27 as follows,

And the kingdom and dominion and the greatness of the kingdom under the whole heaven, shall be given to the people of the saints of the most High whose kingdom is an everlasting kingdom, and all dominions shall serve and obey him.

In Revelation 11, John is told to measure the temple, the altar, and those that worship inside of it, but not to measure the court outside the temple because that area is given to the Gentiles. Verse 2 continues to explain that not only is it that court outside the temple, but also the holy city that will be trampled on for forty-two months. This period of time is three and a half years, significant to end-time events and is mentioned in other prophecies that have been previously studied in this book. In Revelation 12, the woman who is "nourished in the wilderness" is there for three and a half years "away from the face of the serpent." I believe this woman represents the Jewish church that received Jesus as Messiah and birthed the Christian faith.

Contrary to the current notion that the Christian church will be raptured out of any tribulation, I view this vision of Zechariah as insight to help understanding how the Gentile powers will trample Jerusalem at the time of the visitation of the "two witnesses." These powers will persecute the believers in Jesus as the Messiah. These believers are those who I believe to be the "remnant of the seed of the woman" referred to in Revelation 12:17.

Chapter 2 begins with Zechariah's vision of a man with a measuring line, and when Zechariah asks where this man is going, we learn that this man is measuring the dimensions of the city of Jerusalem. In verses 3–5, Zechariah sees an angel talk to another angel who is instructed as such, "Run, speak to this young man, saying, Jerusalem shall be inhabited *as* towns without walls for the multitude of men and cattle therein: For I, saith the Lord, will be unto her a wall of fire round about and will be the glory in the midst of her." So it is the Lord that is speaking to the angel to deliver this message to Zechariah. One has to understand how the triune nature of God comes into play when we are privy to Zechariah's life as we read the words he wrote inspired by the Holy Spirit.

So how are we to understand this vision of the "wall of fire?" Spiritually, I view this as the protection of the Lord. Remember how the Lord demonstrated His presence to the Jews in the wilderness as a "pillar of fire" by night during the Exodus. He gave them security in the darkness of the desert. It seems as though we are living in the darkness of a spiritual desert where God's people are hungry and thirsty for the security of understanding His word and how it applies to them and the world in which they live. The expression "towns without walls" means that there is no limit to the extent of the establishment of communities of believers. All over the world, there are groups of people who have faith in Jesus Christ. We are living in the times of the expression of this vision.

I had a similar personal vision for the city of Tucson, Arizona. In 1995, I saw a vision of the Lord Jesus Christ standing in what I call was a wall of fire. He looked like a man in a white robe and when I asked Him what did this vision mean, He said, "If you want to be in my presence, you will have to go through the fire." Ten years later, as I continue to work on this book, I now I understand what "going through the fire" means.

In 1996, I had a miscarriage. In 1997, I spent eight months in so much pain that I could not sit, stand, or walk for any length of time. In 1998, my husband had a stroke from a rare autoimmune disorder which we were told was incurable and fatal. In 2003, he had to have a quadruple bypass heart surgery. We finally reached a point where we could no longer keep the home we had personally built and had to sell it. He had to give up working because of his disabilities. We were devastated by our financial losses but even more so by the physical challenges the stroke brought about. We have been through the fire spiritually, emotionally, mentally, and physically. Along the way, the Lord has been surrounding us with the burning brilliance of His presence so that even though we "lost it all" as the world may see it, we feel like we have gained it all.

I have come to understand that being in that wall of fire is the blessed assurance of the Lord's deep abiding presence in the midst of complete turmoil. I see personal trials as a prelude to the corporate trial the church will have to face as the days draw closer to the coming of the Lord. Going through our fire burned away all that would be a snare to us. Jesus warned in Luke 21:34–35,

> And take heed to yourselves, lest at any time your hearts be overcharged with surfeiting, and drunkenness, and cares of this life, *and so* that day come upon you unawares. For as a snare shall it come on all them that dwell on the face of the whole earth.

The word surfeiting implies that one is morally seduced, mentally deluded, and/or obsessed with acquiring or paying interest.

How many followers of Jesus Christ are held captive to a lifestyle that cannot afford? How many of us place so much importance on the physical that we neglect the spiritual? How has the enemy deceived the body of Christ, even in the midst of a congregation, to be caught up in the world's systems of belief? Who will accept this fire of God if it means relinquishing all that we hold dear? Who wants to be in His presence so desperately that they would endure whatever that fire might require?

The first martyrs of the faith were able to endure a physical fire because they had the presence of the Holy Fire of God in the person of the Holy Spirit breathing inside of them! Are you willing to renounce this world's system and all its attractions to enter into the consuming fire of the Most High God? I guarantee it will be painful but passing through that wall of fire will bring you into the realm of the Eternal One, the Self-Existent One who upon creation breathed His breath of life into Adam, formed from the clay of the earth.

The ancient Hebrew manuscripts say that man became a "living fire" rather than a "living soul" in Genesis 2:7. This is the breath of life that the Gospel of John calls the life that was the light of the world. Jesus said the life is in the blood of His creation. This life of the Spirit that was stolen by sin was redeemed by the spilling of the blood back onto the earth from the only God–man, Jesus Christ. He gave His life for us so that we could be born again by the fire of His Holy Spirit. We are able to go through the fire when we allow the Holy Spirit to have His full expression in our lives. This can only be possible when we truly surrender all to Him and love Him with all our heart, soul, and strength. We can endure the trial by fire when we have the fire of the Holy Spirit of Jesus in us. We can stand inside that wall of fire where the Lord Jesus is the glory in the midst of us spiritually before He literally is present during the millennial reign and in the New Jerusalem.

> And He shewed me Joshua the high priest standing before the angel of the Lord, and Satan standing at his right hand to resist him, And the Lord said unto Satan, The Lord rebuke thee, O Satan; even the Lord that hath chosen Jerusalem rebuke thee: *is* not this a brand plucked out of the fire? (Zechariah 3:1–2)

Joshua was the high priest at the time that the Lord used Haggai, the prophet, to voice His complaint that the house of the Lord was not built. At the same time, Zerubbabel was the governor of Jerusalem and later when the temple was completed it was known as Zerubbabel's temple. It was the same temple that stood during the ministry of Jesus Christ; however, it was extravagantly remodeled by Herod and of course was called Herod's temple at that time.

Zechariah 3 and 4 tell us about Joshua and Zerubbabel in this fourth vision. We see through this vision that, first of all, Satan is there to resist Joshua, but the Lord rebukes him and describes Joshua as a "brand plucked out of the fire." Notice that it says in chapter 3 verse 2, "And the Lord rebuke thee, O Satan: even the Lord that hath chosen Jerusalem rebuke thee…" The land that Jerusalem occupies is significant. The Lord has appointed these two men to be in charge of the rebuilding of the temple, and immediately, there is the spiritual resistance that we are privy to through Zechariah's vision. Later, in chapter 4, we read the powerful verse that says, "Not by might, nor by power, but by my spirit, saith the Lord of hosts." The visions of chapters 3 and 4 represent the office of the priesthood, which is symbolic for the Messiah, also referred to as the "BRANCH" in chapter 3 verse 8 and the laying of the foundation of the temple with the plummet and the cornerstone in chapter 4 verses 9–10. It is the Lord who will accomplish the work.

Zechariah's vision tells us how the Lord instructs those that were standing by to take away Joshua's dirty clothes and give him clean clothes and a new headdress. This was done to "cleanse Joshua from his sins." In chapter 3 verses 6–7, we read,

> And the angel of the Lord protested unto Joshua, saying, Thus saith the Lord of hosts; If thou wilt walk in my ways, and if thou wilt keep my charge, then thou shalt also judge my house, and shalt also keep my courts and I will give thee places to walk among these that stand by.

Upon reading this verse, I thought of the verse in Hebrews 12:22–23 which describes our access to the heavenly Jerusalem and all those present as "an innumerable company of angels, To the general assembly and church of the firstborn, which are written in heaven, and to God, the Judge of all, and to the spirits of just men made perfect." Once again, we need to see this vision as to how it pertains to the time frame that it was spoken for the actual rebuilding of the temple. Then we need to recognize how the Lord intended to make known that He would be the cornerstone of the temple that would be laid without the hand of man. This represents how He would be the cornerstone, the head of the church, which is His body. In chapter 3 verses 8–9, we read,

> Hear now, O Joshua the high priest, thou, and thy fellows that sit before thee: for they *are* men wondered at: for, behold, I will bring forth my servant the Branch. For behold the stone that I have laid before Joshua; upon one stone *shall* be seven eyes; behold, I will engrave the graving thereof, saith the Lord of hosts, and I will remove the iniquity of that land in one day.

In Zechariah 4:10, we understand that those seven eyes are the eyes of the Lord that search the whole earth. Interestingly, it is the horses in the first vision of Zechariah that are also searching the whole earth or as the Old English translation puts it, "walk to and fro through the earth."

It was the establishment of the high priesthood and the laying of the foundation of the temple, which symbolically gives insight to the establishment of the mediation that Jesus would accomplish as our High Priest. Not only was He our High Priest but he also gave His body as the sacrifice for our sins. His body is compared to the veil and that actual veil was torn even as the body of Christ was torn. It is no accident that the name Jesus comes from the Hebrew word Joshua or otherwise, Yeshua.

The imagery of Joshua being a "brand plucked from the fire" could be compared to a branding iron. Could it be that this is meant to show us how our High Priest, Jesus will brand or mark us by fire? We read in Acts how the Holy Spirit descended like a tongue of fire upon the apostles when they received power from on high. This was a spiritual mark placed on those in the upper room, the believers that were sealed for the day of redemption. Likewise we who receive the baptism of fire are marked or branded by the fire of the Holy Spirit for the day that our redemption "draws nigh."

We could also view this phraseology as describing those who are chosen by the Lord, having been described as a "royal priesthood," who are meant to leave their mark after having been through the fire. Either way, the implication is clear. To be sealed for the day of redemption because the blood of Jesus has cleansed us from our sins, we then become a priest unto the Lord. That priesthood involves a ministering aspect that is seldom mentioned in our day because most attend church to be ministered to, and even though that is an important reason for church attendance, it should not be the only reason. Worship is another way that we minister to Jesus, and when we help those in need, we are essentially ministering to Him.

However, the privilege of ministering to the son of the Most High God as His priest should be something that we do out of love, reverence, and obedience with "godly fear" as written in Hebrews. I know that the times of ministering to the Lord will yield greater understanding and deeper intimacy than can be put into words. We as brands plucked from the fire can even sear His heart with our love for Him and in turn our hearts will burn with a passion that is so desperately needed in our time to reach the lost with His eternal love.

(Since the visions are so crucial to understanding the book of Zechariah, I will give a summation of the remaining four visions before proceeding to the next verse with the word fire in it.)

The fifth vision is found in the fourth chapter in which Zechariah sees a golden candlestick that has seven lamps on it. These seven lamps are being fed oil continuously by two bowls that are being filled through two tubes (called pipes in the Old English version). It is not until Zechariah has asked the angel three times to explain the vision that we learn that the olive trees that are on either side of the candlestick are the source of the oil and the olive trees represent the "two anointed ones that stand by the Lord of the whole earth." It is my opinion that there is a direct connection between this vision of Zechariah and the vision that John describes in the first chapter of Revelation. When John turns to see who was speaking to him, he sees seven golden candlesticks that represent the seven churches "and one like unto the Son of man" standing in the midst of the candlesticks.

It is not until Revelation 11:4 that we read of the two witnesses that are described as "the two olive trees and the two candlesticks standing before the God of the earth." Even though I have heard through many studies of the book of Revelation that the two witnesses are Moses and Elijah, I cannot be certain because of these verses in Zechariah 4:14 and Revelation 11:4. It would be hard to determine based on our own understanding to select two of all those we read of in the Bible to represent the "two anointed ones." Sometimes, I have thought it could be John and Daniel but it's only because it seems to me that Daniel sees John measuring the temple, but that's just a personal notion not something I could say with any certainty.

I believe that the important part of this vision is that the anointed ones pour out of themselves to keep the fires burning on the candles that represent the seven churches and that Jesus is in the midst of those seven churches and has in His hands the seven stars which represent the seven angels of the seven churches. The anointing to the seven churches, the presence of Jesus in those seven churches, and the protection of the seven churches which are directed by the Lord's hand are the important facets of both Zechariah's and John's visions combined.

Although in the middle of Zechariah's vision in chapter 4 we learn of the Lord's intention to lay the foundation of the temple through Zerubbabel, it is Jesus that is the cornerstone on which the church is built. I bring attention to this because it shows that this vision is pertinent to Zechariah's time, the time of Jesus, and our time, and to the end times. It is a vision that is for us and for the Jews because this symbol of the candlestick with seven lamps (fires) on it is the image of a menorah.

The menorah was kept burning to represent continual worship to the Lord in the Jewish temple. Oil has always represented the anointing of the Lord and the anointing is symbolic of the presence of the Holy Spirit. The title of Jesus as the Christ means the anointed one. So could it be that Zechariah's vision of the two olive trees really represents Jesus and the Holy Spirit, the two that stand before the Lord of the whole earth? Just as Jesus was God incarnate, could it be that the Holy Spirit would become incarnate as one of the witnesses and Jesus would be the other? Why would the angel not explain the meaning of the two olive trees until he had first explained the "word of the Lord" to Zerubbabel? (Zechariah 4:6–10)

Living in the day of the Christian church that was birthed from the Jewish faith and awaiting the consummation of the Gentiles and the return of the remnant of the Jewish believers to Jerusalem, I believe that this fifth vision spans the centuries of church history just as Revelation 12 spans the spiritual battles before, during, and after the appearance of the Lord Jesus Christ on earth to establish His church.

In the fifth chapter, the sixth and seventh visions refer to both a "flying roll" and an "ephah." The flying roll is explained to be a curse to any who steals or swears and this roll is intended to burn down the house of "the thief." It's interesting in John 10 we learn of the "thief" that goes into the sheepfold by any other means than through the gate which is representative of Jesus Christ, the shepherd of our souls. The ephah was a container with an equivalency of five quarts. Amos 8:5 tells of an ephah of lesser amounts that was used dishonestly. A lead lid is placed on the ephah, and in the middle of the ephah is a woman that is called wickedness. Zechariah then sees this ephah being carried away by two women that have wings like a stork, considered to be an "unclean" bird to the Hebrews. Their destination is Shinar, an ancient reference to the alluvial plains of Babylon and also the area from where Abraham had his Semitic origins. There, a house is to be built and this ephah is intended to be the base of the structure. The listing of these two visions simultaneously is deliberate to demonstrate that there will be a curse upon the house that is built upon wickedness where the thief is and those who go there are in the practice of stealing and swearing falsely in the name of the Lord.

In Zechariah 5:6, as Zechariah asks the angel what is the ephah, the angel replies, "This *is* their resemblance through all the earth." Revelation 17:5 refers to a woman who has the name on her forehead: MYSTERY, BABYLON THE GREAT, THE MOTHER OF HARLOTS AND ABOMINATIONS OF THE EARTH. Zechariah is being informed of the counterfeit religion that swears falsely in the name of the Lord. When it comes about, it will have its basis in deceitful commerce. It is no coincidence that the information of another house to be built on wickedness follows the vision of the construction of the temple to be built by the Spirit of the Lord. Even though both were built historically in the past, I maintain that this also refers to the end times because the image of the beast in Daniel includes the head of gold, which is a reference to Babylon, modern day Iraq. Jesus, "the stone that is made without hands" causes the whole image to collapse and it is made up of the other dominions that will have their place in end-time fulfillment of prophecies including Persia, now Iran, Greece and both "legs" of the Roman Empire, which are made up of Italy and Turkey.

In the summer of 2005, I heard a story in the news concerning the Greek Orthodox Church and its loss of property in Jerusalem due to sales made to a Jewish-owned company. This caused the removal and replacement of that church's ruling authority in that area. What I found interesting is that the Greek Orthodox Church is responsible to the synod based in Istanbul, Turkey. Historically, when Constantinople made Christianity the state religion, the area he ruled from was then called "The New Rome." Constantinople is modern day Istanbul. Originally, the Roman Empire ruled from Rome, Italy. These two regions make up the two legs of the image that Daniel saw and the feet that were part iron and part clay; elements that will not combine. The ten toes of that feet would represent to me the ten kings in Revelation 17:12–18 which give their power and strength to the beast and hate the whore of Babylon and destroy her according to verse 16. This woman is said to be the great city that rules over all the kings of the earth in verse 18, but it is the Lord that puts it in their hearts to give their powers to the beast to fulfill His will in verse 17.

Could it be that the iron and clay are a reference to religion and commerce? After all, the ephah was originally a clay container and the lid on this container was made of lead. It seems to me that this symbolizes how the commercial involvement of a church would be that which covers the evil within.

The eighth and final visions of Zechariah is of four chariots that emerge from between two mountains of brass found in 6:1. In Daniel 2:31–35 is the description of the image in the dream of Nebuchadnezzar. Verse 32–33 reads. "This image's head *was* of fine gold, his breast and his arms of silver, his belly and his thighs of brass, His legs of iron, his feet part of iron and part of clay." The gold is for the Assyria-Babylonian Empire, the silver representing the Medo-Persian Empire and the brass represents the Grecian Empire. Considering what we just learned from the sixth and seventh vision we can see how each successive kingdom evolves from the former, since the thighs, legs and feet are all connected. Zechariah 9:13–14 reads,

> When I have bent Judah for me, filled the bow with Ephraim, and raised up thy sons, O Zion, against thy sons, O Greece, and made thee as the sword of a mighty man. And the Lord shall be seen over them and his arrow shall go forth as the lightning; and the Lord God shall blow the trumpet and shall go with whirlwinds of the south.

When Zechariah asks what the four chariots with horses of different colors are the angel tells him in chapter 6 verse 5, "These *are* the four spirits of the heavens, which go forth from standing before the Lord of all the earth."

The black and white horses go into the north country and are responsible for quieting the Lord's spirit in the north country. There is no mention of where the gray-white and reddish horses go. However, in the beginning of the book of Zechariah, we read that the Lord is standing among those horses. I have to wonder if this ties into the four horsemen of the apocalypse in Revelation 6:1–8. The first horse is white that goes to conquer, the second horse is red and takes peace away, the third horse is black and deals with unjust scales and the fourth horse is grey and brings death. I heard a pastor say that these four horsemen have already been released. I don't agree with this position. By comparing the order of events in the first part of Matthew 24 and what these horses represent, I am of the opinion that they represent the beginning of the tribulation period. Jesus did say, "When you see these things" that we should look up because He is coming to redeem us.

I have learned that everything means something in the Bible, and if we only take time to pray for the Holy Spirit's understanding rather than our own, we will see what the Lord is trying to show us. I am firmly convinced that the prophecies of Zechariah are for the end times. What is the Lord trying to reveal to us through these eight visions before Zechariah reveals the "burdens of the Lord?" Is there an order of events that will transpire according to these eight visions that relate to the unfolding of the succession of dominions before the Lord comes to interfere in the affairs of men? Zechariah's main message is one of desolation that comes as a result of the rejection of the Shepherd and continued rejection of God's righteous government. Meanwhile, the enemy is continually trying to establish his control over the world, the Lord's people and also desirous of the worship that the Most High God receives.

More than two years after the eight visions, we find Zechariah questioning the Lord regarding the fast of the fifth month and whether or not he should continue the practice. The Lord's response comes as questions in chapter 7 verses 5–7 wondering if their fasts were really done for Him or for themselves. The Lord would rather that all would listen to the words of the prophets. Further on in verses 9–10 it says,

> Thus speaketh the Lord of hosts, saying, Execute true judgment, and shew mercy and compassion every man to his brother: And oppress not the widow, nor the fatherless, the stranger, nor the poor; and let none of you imagine evil against his brother in your heart.

In chapter 6 verse 15 before this transpires, we read the restoration of Jerusalem will occur "if the people will diligently obey the voice of the Lord your God." When the Lord responds to Zechariah's questions and gives instruction, we read in chapter 7 verse 11 that they refused to listen and "pulled away the shoulder and stopped their ears that they should not hear." This is a perfect word picture of how the rebellious react to correction. We read on to realize that because their hearts were as hard as the hardest rock to what the Lord spoke through their prophets that is why the nation of Israel was scattered and their beautiful land was made desolate.

Chapter eight then tells of how the Lord will restore the land, return His people and live with them in Jerusalem. In verse 19, we learn about a type of fast for the different months "shall be to the house of Judah joy and gladness, and cheerful feasts: therefore love the truth and peace." Can you imagine how Zechariah must have felt to have the hope of the restoration of the temple and the joy that would ensue? This is our hope as believers in the return of Jesus to reign on earth during the millennium and in the new heaven and earth after the final judgment. So are we listening to the word of the Lord and what His Holy Spirit is saying to the church today? Are we paying heed to what the prophets are saying?

Prior to the mention of the two burdens, Zechariah questions the Lord if it was necessary to fast. The Lord answers that it is up to the individual, but He is more concerned that His will for His people is that they are just and truthful. It is obedience that He requires. The consequences of their disobedience would result in desolation and are meant to bring about reforms. The Lord is jealous for His people's devotion and desires for His bride to be holy. The former fast will then become a festival. The burdens of the word of the Lord also has insight for the body of Christ that will be alive to see the Lord return to the Mount of Olives as we continue in this pivotal book in the Bible.

> The burden of the word of the Lord in the land of Hadrach, and Damascus *shall be* the rest thereof: when the eyes of man, as of all the tribes of Israel, *shall be* toward the Lord. And Hamath also shall border thereby; Tyrus, and Zidon, through it be very wise. And Tyrus did build herself a strong hold, and heaped up silver as the dust, and fine gold as the mire of the streets. Behold, the Lord will cast her out, and he will smite her power in the sea; and she shall be devoured with fire. (Zechariah 9:1–4)

A brief overview of the towns mentioned is necessary to get a better understanding as to why Zechariah was told to address the "burden of the word of the Lord" to them. Hadrach is mentioned with Damascus although there is no exact location of this town. Hamath is north of Mount Hermon and was once a stronghold city for Solomon according to 2 Chronicles 8:3–4. Jeroboam II, king of Israel, kept Damascus and Hamath for the ten tribes. It was called great by Amos in chapter 6 verse 2 and was conquered by the Assyrians. Samaria joined Hamath in a revolt against the Assyrians in 720 bc. The Assyrians, as recorded in 2 Kings 17:23 and 30, relocated pagan colonies from Hamath to Samaria. Hamath and Syria merged and were ruled by Damascus according to Jeremiah 49:23. Ezekiel 47:15–20 and 48:1 prophesied that restored Israel would reach to the "entering in of Hamath." This region was also considered to be a pass between the mountain ranges that connected inland Syria with the Mediterranean coast.

Tyrus also know as Tyre and is often mentioned with Zidon, also spelled Sidon and was situated in the sea to safeguard against attacks. It was a stronghold for both Joshua and David. The people of Tyre were commercially minded, trafficked by sea with nobility, and established colonies according to Ezekiel 26:15–17 and 27:33. The prophets complained against Tyrus because they sold Jews as slaves to the Greeks. In Zechariah 9:13, we learn that God will raise up Judah against the Greeks, referred to as Javan, considered to be the world power of Hedonism, a philosophy that equates self-seeking pleasure with high moral values. All these towns are mentioned before the Lord destroys Tyrus with fire even though it is situated in the sea. (Further information about Tyrus is in my first book, *Fire in the Bible: Genesis-Daniel*, in the section called Stones of Fire based on Ezekiel 28:11–19.)

Following this verse are four more towns involved in this burden. They are part of five key Philistine cities. Gaza is on the southern boundary of the land of Palestine (the Roman version of the word Philistine) as opposed to the previous cities occupying the northern region. [Of note on a current basis, the Gaza Strip was recently surrendered to the Palestinians as part of the peace process so that no Israelis occupy that land. The hope of less violence in that region has not been realized.] Gaza was assigned to Judah (Joshua 15:47), and even though it was captured by them, the Philistines regained control (Judges 6:4); Dagon was the main idol of Gaza, also called Azzah, and Ashdod. It was in the temple of Dagon that Samson brought down the pillars (Judges 16:23–30). Gaza was the southwestern limit of Solomon's dominion (1 Kings 4:24). And it is written that Hezekiah killed the Philistines to the southernmost gate of Gaza (2 Kings 18:8). The prophet Amos wrote in 1:6–7 of the fiery destruction intended against Gaza because they had taken the Hebrews captive and turned them over to Edom. The Edomites were descendents of Esau and came from his union with the women of Canaan in the mountain ranges of Edom. According to my *Bible Dictionary*, the Horites, also known as cave dwellers, are listed in his genealogy (See Genesis 36:20).

Ashdod is situated between Jaffa and Gaza and its name means fortified place and is also called Azotus in the New Testament (my *Bible Dictionary*). It is another of the five chief Philistine cities. In Joshua 11:21–23, we learn that it was assigned to Judah but not possessed by them. The Philistines returned the Ark of the Covenant to Israel because they believed it caused their idol Dagon to fall over in the temple in Ashdod in 1 Samuel 5:1–8. Its citizens were among those who opposed the rebuilding of the wall around Jerusalem at the time of Nehemiah (Nehemiah 4:7). The Romans rebuilt Ashdod around 55 BC after a long history of being besieged by the Assyrians, the Egyptians, and King Uzziah had who destroyed their wall.

In my *Bible Dictionary*, Ashkelon means the starting point or migration and it was also one of the five main Philistine cites ruled by lords according to Joshua 13:3. It was located twelve miles north of Gaza and its inhabitants worshipped a pagan goddess that had the body of a fish called Derceto. It was under the control of Judah for a short time according to Judges 1:18. Jeremiah, Zephaniah, and Zechariah tell of its destruction with only a remnant of citizens surviving. During the Crusades, it was captured and recaptured but when Sultan Bibars took it in 1270 AD, he covered this harbor town with stones. Its ruins were discovered to have a natural amphitheater created by rocks that faced the sea in the shape of a semicircle.

Ekron was the furthest north of these five important cities of the Philistines. It was assigned to Judah in Joshua 15:45–46 and controlled by that tribe even though the tribe of Dan temporarily inhabited it as written in Joshua 19:43. Eventually, the Philistines regained possession of it. Ekron was the final city to have the Ark of the Covenant before returning it to Israel according to 1 Samuel 5:10. Baal-zebub was worshipped by the Philistine as their main god and was even consulted by Ahaziah, king of Israel, as read in 2 Kings 1:2–16. We find the judgments pronounced against these five cities in Jeremiah 25:15–20, Amos 1–2, Zephaniah 2:4–5, and Zechariah 9:5 and 7. Jeremiah included these cities as those who would drink of the cup of God's wrath. Amos wrote of the destruction by fire to these cities.

Zephaniah 2:4–5 reads,

For Gaza shall be forsaken and Ashkelon a desolation: they shall drive out Ashdod at the noon day, and Ekron shall be rooted up. Woe unto the inhabitants of the sea coast, the nation of the Cherethites! The word of the Lord is against you; O Canaan, the land of the Philistines, I will even destroy thee, that there shall be no inhabitant.

I learned in my *Bible Dictionary* that the Cherethites were the pagans that worshipped the planets and stars who are believed to have migrated from the isle of Crete and lived in the southern portion of Philistia according to 1 Samuel 30:14. The Chemarim were priests of the high places, Baal and of the golden calves at Bethel. Following this verse is the promise for this area to be for the remnant of the house of Judah. Moreover, God promises to visit them and turn away their captivity.

Ashkelon, Gaza, and Ekron will witness the destruction of Tyre and Sidon by fire. Zechariah 9:8 lets us know that the Lord intends to "encamp about mine house because of the army." This gives us an indication of the timing of this judgment by fire. It is when armies surround Jerusalem as we read in Zechariah 12. This is a reference to the end-time events that will cause our Lord to intervene in the affairs of men when He come to stand on the Mount of Olives and creates a great valley from east to west by an earthquake. Just as the verse in Isaiah 9:6 that tells about Jesus, our Prince of peace, comes in the middle of a prophecy about Assyria. In Zechariah 9:9, we read of the humble entry of Jesus on a donkey in the middle of this prophecy directed against the Philistines. We also read in the remainder of chapter 9 and chapter 10 that the Lord has made provision for His remnant.

Zechariah 10:1 reads, "Ask ye of the Lord rain in the time of the latter rain; *so* the Lord shall make bright clouds, and give them showers of rain, to every one grass in the field." Following this verse, we learn of the Lord's complaint against all who trusted in idols and sought advice from diviners. However, the encouragement comes when the Lord shows in the rest of the chapter that He intends to strengthen the hands of His people against their adversary in the end times. The reference to the latter rain is for the second harvest that would occur before the Lord establishes His millennial reign.

I am of the opinion that just as the former rain enabled the first Christians to endure the pain of persecution as the first martyrs so will the later rain enable the saints of the Most High to endure being overcome for a season as written in Revelation 13:7. Notice that the activity that takes place in that chapter is in the sea and coincides with the information of Tyre and Sidon. Also notice in Revelation 20:4 that the only ones who rule with Jesus during the millennium are those who were beheaded for their faith and did not receive the mark of the beast.

I am afraid for the body of Christ that is being lulled into complacency with the soft messages that are meant to build up the congregations and the coffers of the church. We are living in such dangerous times. Knowledge of the Holy One is understanding. Our lives are so consumed with the cares of the world that we rarely are able to receive counsel from the Lord. I am compelled to write because the Lord has afforded me the time to pour over the Word and the lessons to be learned from the history contained within this sacred text. I write to warn the body of Christ. As long as the church allows this escapist notion to permeate its doctrine, the Lord's people could be assuaged in sin. The strong meat of the word is for those who have exercised their senses by it and because they use it are able to discern evil from good. (Hebrews 5:14)

DOORS OPEN TO FIRE

Open thy doors, O Lebanon, that the fire may devour thy cedars. Howl, fir tree; for the cedar is fallen; because the mighty are spoiled: howl O ye oaks of Bashan; for the forest of the vintage is come down. (Zechariah 11:1)

What Zechariah calls his burdens are his understanding of the consequences of the visions that declare God's intent to bring desolation to all the nations that are the enemy of Israel. It is the Lord who will destroy the nations that oppress Judah. The Lord also intends to bring many other nations into His kingdom. The Lord will protect Jerusalem during this time of desolation, but the blessing of restoration is for the future. The main reason for the promised destruction is because of the continual rejection of the One True Shepherd. As a result, the covenant with the nations is broken leaving Israel open to destruction and the hope of unity for Judah and Ephraim is not realized. The Lord's people turn to false prophets, seers, and diviners and so provoke the Lord to anger.

To understand the mindset of the prophets, we have to realize that whatever visions they have seen are as real as if they happened. The visions are seared on the screen of their minds. The word of the Lord is real as if they heard an audible voice whether internally or externally. There is immediacy in the delivery of the word for the recipient of the message to heed the warning. When we view the vision and hear the word of the Lord by reading the pages of this book, we are examining partly in retrospect because we have the advantage of knowing the history as it transpired. However, the danger is in limiting the understanding of the prophetic to a specific time frame. The Bible as a whole has spoken to the centuries specifically and generally.

The verse for this section is a response to the destruction that has transpired in this burden. Zechariah may be using the various types of trees found in this region metaphorically, but upon closer research of the individual species of trees and the Jordan River, we gain a greater illustration. If the entire region were to suffer the destruction and desolation by fire at the hand of the Lord, the forest in this semiarid land would obviously show the results. The cedars of Lebanon were prized in the buildings of temples and palaces but were also used in making mast for ships and also used to carve idols according to my *Bible Dictionary*. So when Zechariah is telling the cedars to howl, could he be using this form of exclamation to mock the pagans who consulted and worshipped these statues? The oaks of Bashan were magnificent trees that get their name from the Hebrew word *el* that means "strong." Was Zechariah personifying a tree to ridicule those who relied on their personal strength instead of the power of the Lord? The fir tree grew with the cedar and was used in the building of temples and ships but also in the making of spears. The fir trees were used in burial grounds in this region. Could Zechariah be trying to emphasize the reality of death that would ensue from the Lord's judgment by using this imagery?

In Zechariah 11:3, we read, "*There is* a voice of the howling of the shepherds; for their glory is spoiled; a voice of the roaring of young lions; for the pride of Jordan is spoiled." At first glance, there seems to be no connection between the howling of the shepherds and the roaring of the young lions. What is the pride of Jordan? Ashes from a forest fire will contaminate the rivers and that is why the shepherds are howling. The pride of Jordan refers to the lions that hid in the bushes along side the Jordan River. These verses reinforce the message of the prophet in a practical but dramatic way.

So finally, why would Lebanon be asked to open its doors? Deuteronomy 1:7 and Joshua 1:4 inform us that Lebanon was the northwest boundary of the promised land. It is in a mountainous region that is covered by snow. The soil in the lower valleys promotes the growth of vines and that explains the reason for the phrase in chapter 11 verse 1, "for the forest of the vintage is come down." Zechariah was using this word picture of this region as having a door to show that the fire from the wrath of God would originate there. It is easy to gloss over a couple of verses as if there was nothing relevant in them. At first, I was inclined to do just that but after a little bit of research the scripture came alive with depth, meaning, and pertinence.

Chapter 11 represents an interlude before the next burden of the word of the Lord as recounted by Zechariah. In this chapter, the Lord is addressing the shepherds of the land who kill their flocks and don't consider themselves guilty. It is the Lord who intends to care for these poor of the flock for the violence done to them. The Lord then tells us through Zechariah that he intends to break two staves to demonstrate how He will break His covenant with all people and the brotherhood between Judah and Israel. He calls these two staves Beauty and Bands.

There is a definite purpose for these names in relation to what they are used to symbolize. The covenant that the Lord made with all people through Abraham was for the land and his descendants. The promise to Abraham was not exclusively to the Jews although it came through Abraham who was from a Semitic race originating in Chaldee, a region in Mesopotamia. That is why when the staff called Beauty is broken, it represents the covenant broken between Yahweh and all people. The second staff called Bands represents Judah and Israel and the breaking of the brotherhood between the two nations that came from the original twelve tribes of Israel. The name Bands is symbolic of the captivity, which the nation of Israel endured. The name Beauty is symbolic of the Bride of Christ, made up of all people. Zechariah is setting the stage for the final burden of the Lord that speaks to all who are of His flock.

A TORCH OF FIRE

In that day will I make the governors of Judah like an hearth of fire among the wood, and like a torch of fire in a sheaf; and they shall devour all the people round about, on the right hand and on the left: and Jerusalem shall be inhabited again in her own place, even in Jerusalem. (Zechariah 12:6)

Zechariah is speaking the word of the Lord to Israel in the twelfth chapter. The phrase "in that day" is used repeatedly through chapters 12, 13, and 14. Concerning the twelfth chapter alone, verses 3–4, 6, 8–9, and 11 use this phrase:

> And in that day will I make Jerusalem a burdensome stone for all people: all that burden themselves with it shall be cut in pieces though all the people of the earth be gathered together against it. In that day, saith the Lord, I will smite every horse with astonishment and his rider with madness: and I will open mine eyes upon the house of Judah, and will smite every horse of the people with blindness. In that day will I make the governors of Judah like an hearth of fire among the wood, and like a torch of fire in a sheaf; and they shall devour all the people round about, on the right hand and on the left: and Jerusalem shall be inhabited again in her own place, *even* in Jerusalem. In that day shall the Lord defend the inhabitants of Jerusalem and he that is feeble among them at that day shall be as David; and the house of David *shall be* as God, as the angel of the Lord before them. And it shall come to pass in that day, *that* I will seek to destroy all the nations that come against Jerusalem…In that day shall there be a great mourning in Jerusalem as the mourning of Hadadrimmon in the valley of Megiddon.

I surmise from this collection of verses a specific order of events that will transpire on "that day" which I believe to be the great day of the wrath of the Lord as spoken of in Revelation 6:17. First, there will be a siege made surrounding Israel. Second, the horses in this attack will be astonished and the riders struck with madness. According to the *King James Bible Word Book*, the word astonished (sometimes written astonied) is derived from an obsolete verb "astone" which means to strike with panic. In the Old English, this word has a much stronger connotation than what our modern language might infer. Third, Jerusalem will be equipped to burn her enemies. Fourth, the feeble will be like David and David will be like God when the Angel of the Lord defends them. Fifth, the families of David, Nathan, Levi, and Shimei, which have been separated, will mourn in Jerusalem. This mourning is referred to in the tenth verse and comes about as the Lord pours "the spirit of grace and of supplications" upon the house of David and those that live in Jerusalem when they look upon the one they "pierced." I wonder why these four families are named. What is there connection and why are they the ones that are singled out as the families that mourn?

Upon studying the names in my *Bible Dictionary*, I learned that Shimei the son of Gershon, the grandson of Levi, as found in Exodus 6:16–17; Numbers 3:18, 21; 1 Chronicles 23:7, 10. Nathan was the third child of David who Luke uses to connect David and Jesus genetically in the ancestral account in chapter 3 verse 31. Levi is also listed as one of the relatives of Jesus on Joseph's side in Luke 3:24 and 29. This is why verse 10 says they will mourn and be in bitterness as for their firstborn when they realized their own ancestors were responsible for the death of Jesus. Those of the House of David, whose ancestors rejected Jesus as their Messiah at His first coming, will have the chance to accept Him as their Messiah at His Second Coming.

The mourning in Jerusalem is compared to the mourning for Hadadrimmon in the valley of Megiddon. My *Bible Dictionary* explains this was the mourning done for King Josiah who was killed at Megiddo during the battle with the army of Pharaoh-nechoh according to 2 Kings 23:29. The word Armageddon means the mountains of Megiddo/Megiddon, and Megiddo means a place of troops. So when Zechariah draws this comparison, he is prophetically revealing that, at the battle of Armageddon, those who mourn in Jerusalem will mourn for the death of Jesus as the one who should have been their king.

Zechariah 12:2 reads, "Behold, I will make Jerusalem a cup of trembling unto all the people round about, when they shall be in the siege both against Judah *and* against Jerusalem." In verse 5, the governors claim that the inhabitants of Jerusalem will be their "strength in the Lord of host their God." Verse 9 declares that the Lord will destroy all the nations that come against Jerusalem. Those that ally themselves with God's chosen people will be protected and strengthened and have God's power to come against their enemies. There is no other way to interpret this as when Jesus returns to gather His own and defend His land. Jesus, who came to His own and His own rejected Him as John wrote of in the first chapter of that gospel, is divinity and humanity portrayed in the One who will return to reign as king in Jerusalem.

REFINED BY FIRE

And it shall come to pass, *that* in all the land, saith the Lord, two parts therein shall be cut off *and* die; but the third shall be left therein. And I will bring the third part through the fire, and will refine them as silver is refined, and will try them as gold is tried: they shall call on my name, and I will hear them: I will say, It *is* my people: and they shall say, The Lord is my God. (Zechariah 13:8–9)

This verse about the refinement of a third of the people comes in the context of the events that transpire "in that day." The phrase "in that day" is used fourteen times in chapters 12, 13, and 14. Each time that phrase is used, we see the Lord's activity "in that day." In chapter 12 verse 3, we read that Jerusalem will become a "burdensome stone" for all people and these people who gathered against her will be cut in pieces. In chapter 12 verse 4, the Lord will strike the horses with "astonishment" and blindness and the riders with madness; chapter 12 verse 6 declares that the governors of Judah will have the ability to burn the enemies that surround them; chapter 12 verse 8 shows that the Lord will defend the inhabitants of Jerusalem; chapter 12 verse 9 says that the Lord will seek to destroy those who come against Jerusalem; chapter 12 verse 11 explains there will be great mourning in Jerusalem; chapter 13 verse 1 begins with telling us that there will be a fountain that will cleanse the sins of the inhabitants of Jerusalem; chapter 13 verse 2 says the Lord will cut off the names of the idols in the land, the false prophets and the unclean spirits; chapter 13 verse 4 tells us those prophets will be ashamed and won't be able to deceive by wearing rough garments.

Chapter 14 begins with, "Behold, the day of the Lord cometh…" describing the time when all nations are gathered against Jerusalem to battle and the Lord stands on the Mount of Olives to fight for her; chapter 14 verse 6 describes the light of that day as being neither clear nor dark; chapter 14 verse 7 goes on to explain: But it shall be one day which shall be known to the Lord, not day, nor night: but it shall come to pass, *that* at evening time it shall be light; chapter 14 verse 8 reveals that living waters will go out from Jerusalem; chapter 14 verse 9 says that the Lord will be king over all the earth as the only Lord and "his name one." For all who came against Jerusalem there will be plagues that consume their flesh, eyes and tongues; chapter 14 verse 13 shows that there will be a "great tumult" from the Lord that will cause neighbors to rise up against each other. Finally, chapter 14 verse 20 reads, "In that day shall there be upon the bells of the horses, HOLINESS UNTO THE LORD; and the pots in the Lord's house shall be like the bowls before the altar."

In compiling these verses, we essentially have an overview of what will occur "in that day." It is the refinement of one third of the people that happens in the middle of all these events. The thirteenth chapter tells us that first there will be a fountain specifically for the house of David, then a purging of the false prophets and unclean spirits before the sword is "awoke" against the shepherd and the sheep are scattered. Often, this verse is used to refer to the time when the Lord was arrested and His followers fled in fear. Perhaps, one could use that comparison. However, I believe its implication for the Day of the Lord is clearly stated within the context of all the verses previously noted. So how does this refinement by fire pertain to the body of Christ now and to those alive before the Lord returns?

This purifying process is what I call the baptism of fire. The verse we are addressing in Zechariah solidifies my belief in the baptism of fire and how it is an integral part of our becoming identified with Christ in His suffering. I believe that believers will individually go through trials by fire, those events in our lives that make us totally dependent on the Lord and burn away all that we don't need. These times of individual refinement are the way the Lord is preparing His people to go through the fire corporately. His bride will be purified before He returns for her.

I first began to wonder about the baptism by fire when I heard a message that said that the baptism of fire was the judgment of hell. I could not agree with that. In Matthew 3:11, John the Baptist said that the One who would come after him would baptize with the Holy Spirit and with fire. Jesus said in Luke 12:49–50, "I am come to send fire on the earth; and what will I, if it be already kindled? But I have a baptism to be baptized with; and how am I straitened [distressed] till it be accomplished!" Jesus refers to this baptism again in Mark 10:38–39 when James and John, the sons of Zebedee, wanted to secure their position on the right and left side of Jesus in His glory. Jesus lets them know their position in heaven would be up to the Father. However, when He asked if they could drink the same cup and receive the same baptism, Jesus was referring to His crucifixion. Unknowingly, James and John replied they could and Jesus let them know they would. If the baptism by water represents the death of the old man as stated in Romans 6, I maintain that the baptism by fire represents the death to self of the new man.

Zechariah 13:9 tells "in all the land" two-thirds of the people will be cut off and one-third will remain to go through the fire.

This reminds me of what Billy Graham once said of all the people who have gone forward at the end of his crusade. Based on the parable of the sower, he knew that only one fourth of those people will spend eternity with Jesus. "In that day," only one-third of all of those who claim to be Christian will endure the refinement by the baptism of fire. They will be the ones that will call on the name of the Holy One of Israel, the Lord Jesus Christ. They will be the ones that say the "Lord is my God." They will be the ones that hear the Lord say, "It is my people."

10

MALACHI

USELESS FIRE

Who *is there* even among you that would shut the doors *for nought?* neither do ye kindle *fire* on mine altar for nought. I have no pleasure in you, saith the Lord of hosts, neither will I accept an offering at your hand. For from the rising of the sun even unto the going down of the same my name *shall be* great among the Gentiles: and in every place incense *shall be* offered unto my name, and a pure offering: for my name *shall be* great among the heathen, saith the Lord of hosts. (Malachi 1:10–11)

According to my *Bible Dictionary*, the name Malachi means either "my messenger" or "messenger of Jehovah." There is some debate as to whether this name is a title or an actual name but since it is used as the title of the book, as were the previous eleven other minor prophets, most agree it was the name of the prophet. Chronologically, this book would follow Haggai and Zechariah because the temple was built and sacrifices were being offered. The estimated time of this book is either 420 or 460–450 BC. The Jews were controlled by a governor most likely appointed by a Persian emperor based on the account in Nehemiah 8.

There are three main sections to this book. The first speaks of the special love that God has for Israel because He chose Jacob over Esau. The second warns of the impending judgment and the third is a call to repentance. Malachi's message decries the lack of devotion from those who were so zealous after their release from Babylonian captivity. He complains of the cruelty among the brethren and their marriages to heathen women and their propensity to divorce. He also addresses the corruption of the priesthood and the dishonoring of God with their imperfect sacrifices.

In the beginning of the first chapter, it is written as if a father is writing to a son. The second chapter is addressed to the priesthood and to the "masters and the scholars." Chapter 2 ends with the sad statement: Ye have wearied the Lord with your words. Yet ye say, Wherein have we wearied *him*? Every one that doeth evil *is* good in the sight of the Lord, and he delighteth in them; or Where *is* the God of judgment?

It's as if the Lord's forbearance causes them to rail against Him and question His authority. How impertinent and impenitent were the people and priests of Malachi's day. Yet, in my heart, I know that I have done the same thing. How many times have I wept at the altar of the Lord going on and on about what I thought was unfair? How many times have I run into the throne room of grace and pleaded with God to help me out of some predicament I have gotten into because I wanted my will and not His? How many blemished sacrifices have I presented to the Lord that were tainted with a self-seeking agenda. How many times have I come to the house of the Lord with sin hidden in my heart? How many ultimatums have I given the sovereign Lord of the universe?

I came to a cold, hard reckoning one day. I remember I was sitting on a bench that my husband and I used to put on and take off our shoes. I slipped my feet into my husband's shoes and thought of an old saying about never really knowing what someone is going through until you've walked a mile in their shoes. That day was the third day after he had had open heart surgery, and I had been told to go home and rest. He had already been dealing with so many physical ailments from having suffered a brain stem stroke that we believe was caused by pesticide exposure even though he was diagnosed with a disease that has similar symptoms. Before the heart surgery, he had learned to walk and talk again, but he never regained the feeling on the right side of his face. It's a source of great sadness that his grandchildren have never seen his real smile, and one time, our grandson drew him with one eye because he has to tape his eye shut. He's also developed serious kidney problems because of all the medications he took, and at one point, we were told to prepare for dialysis or a transplant. I sat on that bench remembering that just a few months before I told the Lord to either heal my husband or take him home.

All of a sudden, the Holy Spirit convicted me and I was shocked at my insolence by having given God an ultimatum. Who was I to decide when my husband should go to be with Jesus? I spiritually had to repent in dust and ashes for my impudence. I truly had wearied the Lord with my words, offended Him by telling Him what to do. Four years later, I praised the Lord He didn't listen to my requests. My husband recovered from that surgery and continues to serve the Lord with a powerful witness of how God uses physical trials by fire.

My husband loves to tell this story about how a three-year-old learned to pray from him. One time at a birthday party, my husband was praying for our meal. When his right eye is not taped, it won't close when he shuts his other eye. Later, this little girl's mommy shared with us that one night she saw her daughter praying with one eye open. Often, John has been able to reach out to other people with physical problems and share how the Lord has helped him. He would tell you that all that he's been through has made him a better man and drawn him closer to the Lord. We still hold to the promise the Lord gave us when he first had the stroke. Many are the afflictions of the righteous but the Lord will deliver him from all of them. (Psalm 34:19)

We are told in Romans 12 to present our bodies as a living sacrifice. We become holy and acceptable offerings by the blood of Jesus. The offering of ourselves becomes purified by the trials of fire we endure. Paul wrote, as I repeat: I beseech you therefore, by the mercies of God, that ye present your bodies a living sacrifice, holy, acceptable unto God, *which* is your reasonable service.

Malachi spoke for the Lord to warn his people as he warns us today to bring a pure and undefiled offering to the Lord. The fire that the Lord uses will not be used for "nought." There is divine providence in all that the Lord allows in our lives. Through it all, we can offer Him the "fruit of our lips" giving Him praise for He is worthy. In this, we bring honor and glory to the name of Jesus among those who have yet to believe.

ABIDING IN THE REFINER'S FIRE

Behold, I will send my messenger, and he shall prepare the way before me: and the Lord whom ye seek, shall suddenly come to his temple, even the messenger of the covenant, whom ye delight in: behold, he shall come, saith the Lord of hosts. But who may abide the day of his coming? and who shall stand when he appeareth? for he *is* like a refiner's fire, and like fullers' soap: And he shall sit *as* a refiner and purifier of silver: and he shall purify the sons of Levi, and purge them as gold and silver, that they may offer unto the Lord an offering in righteousness. (Malachi 3:1–3)

The interesting phrase in the verses we are considering is "the messenger of the covenant." Malachi is addressing the Levitical priesthood that will withstand the purifying process. The covenant made with them is referred to in chapter 2 verse 4 where the Lord promises them life and peace because they feared Him. In verses 5–7, we read of the other requirements of the priesthood. The law of truth was to be in their mouths and no iniquity in their lips. They were to walk with the Lord in peace and equity and turn away from iniquity. Verse 7 reads, "For the priest's lips should keep knowledge, and they should seek the law at his mouth for he *is* the messenger of the Lord of hosts." However, in verse 8, we learn they departed from the way and caused many to stumble. They corrupted the covenant of Levi and profaned the covenant of their fathers. Numbers 25:1–18 tells the story of what prompted the Lord to establish the covenant of an everlasting priesthood with Phinehas, the son of Eleazar, the son of Aaron. Israel was cursed with a plague for joining with Baal-peor in marriage and in their worship of pagan deities. Moses told the judges to slay all who did so. Phinehas simultaneously speared a man of Israel and a woman of Midian who were together in a tent. Twenty-four thousand died from the plague. Verse 13 explains that Phinehas was zealous for his God and had made atonement for the children of Israel.

My *Bible Dictionary* states in the definition of covenant that perhaps the Old and New Testament should have been called the Old and New Covenants. In the Old Covenant, the priests and high priests had to be born from the tribe of Levi. In the New Covenant, we who have had our sins washed by the blood of Jesus are called kings and priest to God, His Father, in Revelation 1:5–6. The purpose of the refiner's fire and fuller's soap in chapter 3 is so the "offerings in righteous" will be reinstated as written in verses 3 and 4.

Once again, we see how the priest of Malachi's day had the audacity to question God. When God asked why they have robbed Him, in chapter 3 verse 8, they retort that they have not robbed God by their failure to bring tithes. In chapter 3 verses 13–17, they defensively argue with God when He asks them why they have spoken so harshly to Him. In verses 14–15, they tempt God by saying there is no profit in keeping His ordinances or in walking mournfully before the Lord of hosts. They test the Lord further by claiming the proud are happy and those that tempt God are delivered. How did it get to the place where the creation could speak so rudely to their creator? It sounds all too familiar when we consider the dialogue of atheists, the compromises being made in some churches and what is considered entertainment in our culture.

By contrast, those who fear the Lord and think upon His name will be put in a "book of remembrance" and be like jewels according to verse 16. In verse 17, the Lord promises to spare them and they will be the ones who will discern between the righteous and the wicked. They will be spared from the fire that "burns like an oven" which turns the wicked into ashes on the soles of the feet of the righteous. Malachi ends with the reminder to remember the Law of Moses. We are told the prophet Elijah will turn the "heart of the fathers to the children, and the heart of children to their fathers," or else the Lord will "smite the earth with a curse."

It is no coincidence that both Zechariah and Malachi made references to purification by fire similar to the refining by silver and gold in which all the impurities are removed. Likewise, when the fuller's soap was used, there was pressure put on the material being cleansed to remove all the stains. The Lord is returning for a pure and spotless bride. The body of Christ must be willing to abide in the refiner's fire. This spiritual fire will burn away all the impurities that have seeped into the church before the world and the wicked endure the physical fire written of by Malachi in the final prophetic book in the Old Testament.

11

MATTHEW

I indeed baptize you with water unto repentance: but he that cometh after me is mightier than I, whose shoes I am not worthy to bear: he shall baptize you with the Holy Ghost and *with* fire: Whose fan *is* in his hand, and he will thoroughly purge his floor, and gather his wheat into the garner; but he will burn up the chaff with unquenchable fire. (Matt. 3:11–12)

These verses sparked my desire to understand what the Fire of God is all about and so the journey continues into the New Testament. John the Baptist was from the priestly line of Aaron. His father Zacharias and his mother Elisabeth were both from that tribe. Elisabeth was a cousin to Mary, the mother of Jesus, who was from the tribe of Judah. Luke lists these genealogies in chapter 1 verse 5. In Luke 1:8–17, we learn of the circumstances surrounding the announcement of John's birth. The Angel Gabriel appeared to Zacharias as he was burning incense in the holy of holies and said that John would be filled with the Holy Spirit from his birth and would prepare the way before the Lord.

According to my *Bible Dictionary*, John was born in 5 BC and lived in the wilderness near his home west of the Dead Sea. He began his public ministry in 26 AD believed by some to be a Sabbatic year when the Jews rested from their labor in the fields. This allowed them to spend time listening to John's preaching. John's message was meant to prepare the people's minds and hearts to receive Jesus as the Messiah. He spoke boldly of repentance because the kingdom of God was close at hand. John baptized in the Jordan River all those who confessed their sins. Even though John considered himself inferior to Jesus, still Jesus asked to be baptized by John as told in the third chapter of Matthew. This is where we learn from John that Jesus will baptize all who believe with the Holy Spirit and with fire.

In Matthew 11:7–15, we read how Jesus described John the Baptist. Jesus began to say unto the multitudes concerning John,

> What went ye out into the wilderness to see? A reed shaken with the wind? But what went ye out for to see? A man clothed in soft raiment? Behold, they that wear soft *clothing* are in kings' houses. But what went ye out for to see? A prophet? Yea, I say unto you and more than a prophet. For this is *he* of who it is written, Behold, I send my messenger before thy face, which shall prepare thy way before thee. Verily I say unto you, Among them that are born of women there hath not risen a greater than John the Baptist: notwithstanding he that is least in the kingdom of heaven is greater than he. And from the days of John the Baptist until now the kingdom of heaven suffereth violence, and the violent take it by force. For all the prophets and the law prophesied until John. And if ye will receive *it* this is Elias, which was for to come. He that hath ears to hear, let him hear.

Jesus challenges his listeners to see John as Elias, otherwise known as Elijah. We are told in Malachi 4:5–6, "Behold I will send you Elijah the prophet before the coming of the great and dreadful day of the Lord: And he shall turn the heart of the fathers to the children, and the heart of the children to their fathers, lest I come and smite the earth with a curse." John the Baptist denied that he was Elijah in John 1:21–23 and quoted Isaiah 40:3 when he said: I *am* the voice of one crying in the wilderness, Make straight the way of the Lord, as said the prophet Esaias. How do we reconcile this?

Just as Jesus challenged Nicodemus to understand what being born again meant in John 3, we need to discern these heavenly things spiritually. How do we understand the difference between being baptized in water and also being baptized by fire? Clearly, these are two different things. Why would John the Baptist speak of those from the root of Abraham being cut off and burned and of the wheat being gathered and the chaff also being burned within the context of these verses dealing with these different types of fire?

In Matthew 3:7–10, John the Baptist challenged the Pharisees and Sadducees who came to see the baptism to bring "fruits meet for repentance." John warned there was an axe at the root of the tree of their genealogy if they didn't bear fruit. The religious leaders believed they were in right standing with God by being descendants of Abraham and by observing their rituals. John the Baptist said God could raise up stones as descendants of Abraham. If the religious leaders submitted to baptism, that would mean they needed to repent and be cleansed. The fire that would burn the unrepentant tree symbolized God's way of dealing with spiritual pride and exclusivity.

On the other hand, just as one comes to the waters of baptism and dies to the old man, I believe the baptism of fire is for the new man. This is a process of purification as we learn to deny ourselves, take up our cross, and follow Jesus every day. It encompasses the act of being a living sacrifice. It brings us to an intimacy with Jesus, who is the One who will baptize us with fire spiritually, if we are willing to allow Him to burn away all that would stand in the way. To be in the presence of God who is an "all consuming fire" requires that we submit to this process. This intimacy brings the unity that Jesus prayed for at the Last Supper in John 17:21.

In Matthew 3:12, the unquenchable fire burns up the chaff from the harvest. It is the Lord that is involved in this harvest because the verse says that He will thoroughly purge His threshing floor with the fan in His hand and gather His wheat in the garner. I see this as representing the rapture of the church because chaff is what is left behind. The threshing floor is the Temple Mount that David bought for the site of Solomon's temple. Second Peter 3:10–12 says on the day of Lord the heavens will dissolve, the elements will melt, and fire will burn the earth.

The incarnation of Jesus as the Lamb of God was not before the great and dreadful day of the Lord, but He did usher in the kingdom of God, spiritually. The return of Jesus as the Lion of Judah will usher in the kingdom of God, physically too. This is another example of near and far fulfillment. This is how we understand that John the Baptist operated with the spirit of Elijah. What was the spirit of Elijah? It was the Spirit that called fire down from heaven as written of in 1 Kings 18:38. It was the Spirit that received Elijah with horses and chariots of fire as told in 2 Kings 1:11. It was the work of the Holy Spirit that was with John the Baptist since the day he was born. It was the cleansing that began with water and continued with Jesus leaving us His Holy Spirit. It is the fire that will burn spiritually before the Second Coming of Christ. The fire that purifies spiritually is meant to prepare us to be in the presence of the Holy Fire of God.

> Then Jesus sent the multitude away, and went into the house: and his disciples came unto him, saying, Declare unto us the parable of the tares of the field. He answered and said unto them, He that soweth the good seed is the Son of man; the field is the world; the good seed are the children of the kingdom; but the tares are the children of the wicked *one*; The enemy that sowed them is the devil: the harvest is the end of the world; and the reapers are the angels. As therefore the tares are gathered and burned in the fire; so shall it be in the end of this world. The Son of man shall send forth his angels, and they shall gather out of his kingdom all things that offend, and them which do iniquity; And shall cast them into a furnace of fire: there shall be wailing and gnashing of teeth. Then shall the righteous shine forth as the sun in the kingdom of their Father. Who hath ears to hear, let him hear. (Matthew13:36–43)

Jesus spoke to the multitudes the parable of the tares that begins in Matthew 13:24. Jesus begins by explaining that the kingdom of heaven is like a man that sows good seed in his field. While the man was sleeping the enemy sows the tares, which are also called "weeds" in other translations. In verse 30, Jesus said the weeds should be allowed to grow with the wheat until the time of harvest when they will be burned in the "furnace of fire." If the weeds were pulled up, it would destroy the harvest. When we despair of the evil in this world, we can look at this parable for understanding.

In Matthew 13, Jesus also spoke of the kingdom of heaven in these other parables: the sower; the mustard seed; the leaven; the buried treasure; costly pearl; the large net; the householder's treasure. In Verse 10, when the disciples asked why He spoke in parables, Jesus answered in verse 13 by saying, "Therefore speak I to them in parables: because they seeing see not; and hearing they hear not, neither do they understand." Verse 14 reveals that this was the fulfillment of the prophecy of Isaiah 6:9. Later, when Jesus spoke to his disciples privately, He quotes Psalm 78:2 in Matthew 13:35 when He said, "That it might be fulfilled which was spoken by the prophet saying I will open my mouth in parables; I will utter things which have been kept secret from the foundation of the world." How amazing it was for the disciples to have Jesus reveal these secrets about the kingdom of heaven.

Specifically, in the verses with the word fire in them, Jesus shows that the harvest is indicative of the "end of the world" in Matthew 13:39. The tares are being allowed to grow until the wheat is ready for the harvest. The fire of judgment is reserved for those weeds that "offend" and "do iniquity" as found in verse 40. Consider the impact of the revealing of this "secret" to the disciples as they were privately gathered around Jesus.

I'm sure they all came to Him with the expectation of Him riding their world of all the evil they endured. We too place those expectations on the Lord when we wail against the wickedness in this world. Romans 9:22–24 clarifies,

> *What* if God, willing to show *his* wrath, and to make his power known, endured with much longsuffering the vessels of wrath fitted to destruction. And that he might make known the riches of his glory on the vessels of mercy, which he had afore prepared unto glory, Even us, whom he hath called, not of the Jews only but also of the Gentiles?

I can hear the protest of the unbelievers asking how could God, the Father inflict such horrible punishment. I say, how could He not. For thousands of years, He has endured seeing the effects of sin. He sent His Son to endure the pain of dying on the cross to wipe away that sin for those who would receive Him. Even worse, imagine the moment of separation the Father and Son endured when Jesus was full of our sins. Imagine how God must have felt to hear Jesus cry out, "Why have you forsaken me?" only to see Him die a horrible death. Consider how God felt to see all His prophets, kings, judges, and followers be ignored, mocked, and killed. All along, He has been ignored, cursed, mocked, and rebelled against. It will surprise the evil ones, yet those that love God will understand. Justice will be served. The wicked weeds are doomed to the furnace of fire. Vengeance belongs to the Lord who will repay those who have rejected their own salvation because they loved living in the darkness of their sin rather than living in the light of His holiness.

FALLING INTO THE FIRE

And when they were come to the multitude, there came to him a *certain* man, kneeling down to him, and saying, Lord, have mercy on my son: for he is lunatic, and sore vexed: for oftimes he falleth into the fire, and oft into the water. And I brought him to thy disciples, and they could not cure him. Then Jesus answered and said, O faithless and perverse generation, how long shall I be with you? How long shall I suffer you? Bring him hither to me. And Jesus rebuked the devil; and he departed out of him: and the child was cured from that very hour. Then came the disciples to Jesus apart, and said, Why could not we cast him out? And Jesus said unto them, Because of your unbelief: for verily I say unto you, If ye have faith as a grain of mustard seed, ye shall say unto this mountain, Remove hence to yonder place; and it shall remove; and nothing shall be impossible unto you. Howbeit this kind goeth not out but by prayer and fasting. (Matthew 17:14–21)

I have to wonder why it was important to Matthew to let us know that the man threw himself into the water and into the fire. He only needed to inform us that he was considered a lunatic and was "sore vexed." Perhaps this man with a "devil," inadvertently trying to free himself of the demon in the physical realm, recognized the importance of water and fire. Water in baptism symbolizes our spiritual death of the old man and resurrection into the new life of being born again. I believe the baptism by fire is the crucifying of the new man.

Jesus rebuked his disciples, explaining their lack of faith as the reason they were not able to cure the man's son. Even though the Lord's frustration came with harsh word, He let the disciples know that prayer and fasting were the only way to rid the man of the "devil." As much as I know about the power behind prayer and fasting, I often use it as a last resort. Most of us would admit how hard it is to stay focused when we pray and how hard it is to fast. It seems like those are the times we are most distracted and tempted. That shouldn't come as any surprise. The enemy doesn't want us to realize our potential in the spirit when we take authority over the mind and the flesh.

EVERLASTING FIRE

Woe unto the world because of offences! For it must needs be that offences come; but woe to that man by whom the offence cometh! Wherefore if thy hand or thy foot offend thee, cut them off, and cast *them* from thee: it is better for thee to enter into life halt or maimed, rather than having two hands or two feet to be cast into everlasting fire. And if thine eye offend thee, pluck it out, and cast *it* from thee: it is better for thee to enter into life with one eye, rather than having two eyes to be cast into hell fire. (Matthew 18:7–9)

And if thy hand offend thee cut it off: it is better for thee to enter into life maimed, than having two hands to go into hell, into the fire that never shall be quenched: Where their worm dieth not, and the fire in not quenched. And if thy foot offend thee, cut it off: it is better for thee to enter halt into life, than having two feet to be cast into hell, into the fire that never shall be quenched: Where their worm dieth not, and the fire is not quenched. And if thine eye offend thee, pluck it out: it is better for thee to enter into the kingdom of God with one eye, than having two eyes to be cast into hell fire: Where their worm dieth not, and the fire is not quenched. (Mark 9:43–48)

Immediately preceding these verses in both Gospels, Jesus warns of offending little ones and comparing those that do to be better off if they were drowned by having a "millstone" hung around their neck. In Matthew's version, it is followed by verses 10–11, "Take heed that ye despise not one of these little ones; for I say unto you, That in heaven their angels do always behold the face of my Father which is in heaven. For the Son of man is come to save that which was lost." In Mark's version, we read at the end, "For every one shall be salted with fire, and every sacrifice shall be salted with salt. Salt is good: but if the salt have lost his saltness, wherewith will ye season it? Have salt in yourselves and have peace one with another."

Why would Jesus use such graphic descriptions as recorded by Matthew and Mark? I believe it is to speak of the gravity of the sin in allowing our flesh to determine our eternal destiny. When we think of it literally, anything physical that causes us to sin should be cut off from our life. I believe if we go to places that are sinful, it would be better not to be able to walk than to sin. If we are involved in any endeavor, the work of our hands, that is sinful, if would be better not to be able to work with our hands. And if we chose to view those things that are sinful, it would be better to be blind.

Jesus has a definite purpose in following His warning against offending little ones with these illustrations of removing our eye, hand, or foot if it leads us into sin. Consider the immense influence every adult has on each child. If these little ones are never offended by witnessing such sins, they might not be influenced to do the same. I believe the reason why in Matthew's account Jesus goes even further to let us know that the angels of the little ones are looking upon our Father God is to further our understanding of the impact of offenses not only physically but spiritually.

Mark's version includes the intense finality of hell by describing it as a place where the worm never dies and the fires are never quenched. Without the hope of eternal life, we have the grave image of being consumed forever by worms and fire. So in comparison, being maimed would be better if it prevented us from following a lifestyle of sin rather than suffer forever.

In Mark's version, the chapter concludes with Jesus explaining that everyone will be salted with fire and every sacrifice shall be salted with salt. Salt was not only used in His time as a preservative but also to cleanse. When a child was born it was cleansed by rubbing the body with salt then oil. What does Jesus mean by saying everyone will be "salted with fire?"

In Leviticus 2:13 it reads,

> And every oblation of thy meat offering shalt thou season with salt; neither shalt thou suffer the salt of the covenant of thy God to be lacking from thy meat offering: with all thine offering thou shalt offer salt.

In Ezekiel 43:23–24, we read,

> When thou hast made an end of cleansing *it*, thou shalt offer a young bullock without blemish, and a ram out of the flock without blemish. And thou shalt offer them before the Lord, and the priests shall cast salt upon them and they shall offer them up *for* a burnt offering unto the Lord.

Salt was an intrinsic element of the sacrifice under the law so much so that there was "the salt of the covenant of thy God" to be used continually and perpetually as found in Leviticus 2:13. Numbers 18:19 says,

> All the heave offerings of the holy things, which the children of Israel offer unto the Lord, have I given thee, and thy sons and thy daughters with thee, by a statute for ever: it is a covenant of salt for ever before the Lord unto thee and to thy seed with thee.

Second Chronicles 13:5 reads, "Ought ye not to know that the Lord God of Israel gave the kingdom over Israel to David for ever, *even* to him and to his sons by a covenant of salt?" Did you notice that the "little ones" are included in these verses? My *Key Word Study Bible* explains this and I quote, "Eating salt together signified an unbreakable friendship." Salt was used as a preservative. Therefore, it was an appropriate symbol for eternity. A covenant of salt could not be changed.

In my *Bible Dictionary*, part of the definition for salt reads: Salt preserves from corruption and renders food palatable, and is therefore used figuratively for the true disciples of Jesus, who by their precepts and example raise the moral tone of society (Matthew 5:13; Mark 9:50; Luke 14:34). When we have made our lives a living sacrifice, as the book of Romans tells us to, being "salted with fire" will purify us. This spiritual sacrifice will burn away those tendencies to sin. The salt in us influences the world around us. Most importantly, we enter into an eternal covenant that preserves us from the everlasting fire.

PREPARED FIRE

> When the Son of man shall come in his glory, and all the holy angels with him, then shall he sit upon the throne of his glory: And before him shall be gathered all nations: and he shall separate them one from another, as a shepherd divideth *his* sheep from the goats: And he shall set the

> sheep on his right hand, but the goats on the left. Then
> shall the King say unto them on his right hand, Come,
> ye blessed of my Father, inherit the kingdom prepared
> for you from the foundation of the world…Then he shall
> say also unto them on the left hand, Depart from me, ye
> cursed, into everlasting fire, prepared for the devil and his
> angels. (Matthew 25:31–34, 41)

Jesus explains why those on His left are sent to everlasting fire in verses 42–45:

> For I was an hungered, and ye gave me no meat; I was
> thirsty, and ye gave me no drink: I was a stranger, and
> ye took me not in: naked, and ye clothed me not: sick,
> and in prison, and ye visited me not. Then shall they also
> answer him, saying Lord, when saw we thee an hungered
> or athirst or a stranger, or naked or sick, or in prison, and
> did not minister unto thee? Then shall he answer them,
> saying Verily I say unto you, Inasmuch as ye did *it* not to
> one of the least of these ye did *it* not to me.

This response is the opposite reply He gave to those on His right found in verses 35–40. Those on His right and left have one thing in common they both address Jesus as Lord. This alone should get the attention of every born again believer. James 2:18 reads, "Yea, a man may say, Thou hast faith, and I have works: shew me thy faith without thy works, and I will shew thee my faith by my works." Also, James 2:26 reads, "For as the body without the spirit is dead, so faith without works is dead also."

I am reminded of the vision I saw of the Lord's hand going into a fountain, and as He did, the water ran through the hole in His hand. I asked Him what did it mean and He said that His people had not bound up His wounds. I asked Him what I could do and He said, "The acceptable fast." Isaiah wrote in chapter 58 to care for the hungry, poor, naked, and those in our own families that need help rather than denying ourselves. The "acceptable fast" also includes releasing those that are held captive by wickedness, oppression, and heavy burdens. Individually and corporately, we could spend a lifetime ministering to these needs.

Another interesting thing to notice is found in verse 32 where we read it is *all* the nations that are gathered. At first, I wondered if this meant the nations would be separated to the right and left side of Jesus. What if the nations came under judgment at that time? If that were the case it would mean the Lord's return would be when the nations are gathered as written of in Isaiah 66. Starting in verse 14, we learn the Lord's hand "shall be known to his servants, and *his* indignation toward his enemies" when the Lord comes with fire. Verse 18 explains, "For I *know* their works and their thoughts: it shall come, that I will gather all nations and tongues; and they shall come, and see my glory."

Could these two accounts refer to the same time? It is the Lord that gathers the nations to see His glory and to judge their works. Zechariah 12 also tells of the time when the Lord gathers all nations against Jerusalem to battle. Is it possible this would refer to the same event?

In both Isaiah and Zechariah there is a restoration of Jerusalem to be "safely inhabited" according to Zechariah 12:11 and in Isaiah 66:23–24 we read,

> And it shall come to pass, *that* from one new moon to another, and from one Sabbath to another, shall all flesh come to worship before me saith the Lord. And they shall go forth, and look upon the carcases of the men that have transgressed against me: for their worm shall not die, neither shall their fire be quenched; and they shall be an abhorring unto all flesh.

Clearly, this is a reference to the everlasting fire. I also believe this separation of the sheep and the goats, both plural analogies, points to the time before the millennial reign of Christ rather than after the final judgment because there will be no moon or sun in the new heaven and earth.

Zephaniah 3:8–9 reads,

> Therefore wait ye upon me, saith the Lord, until the day that I rise up to the prey: for my determination *is* to gather the nations, that I may assemble the kingdoms, to pour upon them mine indignation, *even* all my fierce anger: for all the earth shall be devoured with fire of my jealousy. For then will I turn to the people a pure language, that they may all call upon the name of the Lord, to serve him with one consent.

Furthermore, Zechariah 2:11 says, "And many nations shall be joined to the Lord in that day, and shall be my people: and I will dwell in the midst of thee, and thou shalt know that the Lord of hosts hast sent men unto thee."

12

MARK

> And they led Jesus away to the high priest: and with him were assembled all the chief priests and the elders and the scribes. And Peter followed him afar off, even into the palace of the high priest: and he sat with the servants, and warmed himself by the fire. (Mark 14:53–54)

In this chapter, we are told the events surrounding the story of how Peter denied the Lord three times. This is also recorded in Luke 22 and Matthew 26. In Mark 14:27–28, Jesus said that all of them would be offended because of Him. Peter argued that he would not, but Jesus said he would deny Him three times before the cock crowed twice. In Luke 22:31–34, we read that Jesus spoke these words before Peter said he would be willing to go to prison and even die for Him, "Simon, Simon, behold, Satan hath desired *to have* you, that he may sift *you* as wheat: But

I have prayed for thee that thy faith fail not: and when thou art converted, strengthen thy brethren."

In both accounts, this event happens after they had observed the Passover, which is now referred to as the Last Super. Mark writes that Peter said he would not be offended of Jesus while they were at the Mount of Olives. Luke wrote of Peter willing to be imprisoned and die for Jesus before they went to the Mount of Olives. In Mark 14:31, we read that Peter spoke vehemently that even if he would die, he would not deny Jesus and all the rest said the same thing before they went to the Mount of Olives. When I first noticed this difference, I thought it was a contradiction. On second thought, what if Peter said he wouldn't deny the Lord once before they went to the Mount of Olives and twice while there before he actually did deny Him three times publicly?

Jesus told Peter He would pray for him right before he was about to reject the notion for the third time. In contrast, Peter is the only one named when Jesus found the disciples sleeping after He had asked them to pray with Him because His soul was "sorrowful even unto death." No wonder Jesus also said the spirit was willing but the flesh weak in Matthew 26:41. It's important to notice that Jesus called Peter Simon and said that name twice for emphasis. Peter had such boldness even to the point of contradicting the Lord to His face before his test of faith came. I can't help but be convicted by this. What if I live to see the day that I must deny Christ or die? I know that in and of myself, I have no strength to remain faithful under such persecution. That's why I firmly believe that the outpouring of the Holy Spirit in the last days will be greater for that specific reason. The latter rain will be greater than the former rain because believers in the last days will endure greater persecution than the first believers.

Once Jesus was captured, Peter followed him from afar. Reading in Mark 14:66–72, I wonder what he was thinking as he stood there warming his hands over the fire. Did his heart burn with fear for what might happen next? Why did he curse and swear on his third denial? He wasn't the only who said he wouldn't deny Christ. The others ran away. Peter wept after the cock crowed because it wasn't until then that he thought about what Jesus had said. Imagine the fire of conviction that would burn in his spirit. Satan had sifted his faith because he had boasted in the weakness of his flesh. Jesus prayed that his faith would not fail because he would have to strengthen the other disciples after he was converted according to Luke 22:32.

Dwell on what that process must have meant for Peter. Consider the sovereignty of God in the midst of all of this. Peter could not have known how to be bold by the power of the Holy Spirit until he had failed in the flesh. He could have chosen to be stifled by remorse, but he didn't and so we can look to Peter when we have failed the Lord. How else could he have written in 1 Peter 1:6–7,

> Wherein ye greatly rejoice, though now for a season, if need be, ye are in heaviness through manifold temptations; That the trial of your faith, being much more precious than of gold that perisheth, though it be tried with fire, might be found unto the praise and honour and glory at the appearing of Jesus Christ.

13

LUKE

And it came to pass, when the time was come that he should be received up, he stedfastly set his face to go to Jerusalem, And sent messengers before his face: and they went, and entered into a village of the Samaritans, to make ready for him. And they did not receive him, because his face was as though he would go to Jerusalem. And when his disciples James and John saw *this*, they said, Lord wilt thou that we command fire to come down from heaven, and consume them, even as Elias did? But he turned, and rebuked them, and said, Ye know not what manner of spirit ye are of. For the Son of man is not come to destroy men's lives, but to save *them*. And they went to another village. (Luke 9:51–56)

Why would James and John want to bring fire down like Elijah? (Spelled Elias in the Old King James version.) The history of

Samaria brings insight to this story. Samaria was the capital of the northern kingdom and was known for its idolatry that Elijah had prophesied against. In 1 Kings 18–19, Elijah had killed the prophets of Baal after calling down fire to consume a sacrifice. He had fled from the threats of Jezebel and was in a cave when the Lord calmed him with His "still small voice." He commanded him to anoint Jehu king over Israel. In 2 Kings 9, we read that Elisha accomplished this for Elijah by sending the "children of the prophets" to anoint Jehu with oil and proclaim him to be king. In verses 6 to 7, we read the word of the Lord as given by this young man,

> Thus saith the Lord God of Israel, I have anointed thee king over the people of the Lord, *even* over Israel. And thou shalt smite the house of Ahab thy master, that I may avenge the blood of my servants the prophets, and the blood of all the servants of the Lord, at the hand of Jezebel.

Chapters 9 to 10 recount how Jehu killed Jehoram, Ahab's son and Ahaziah whose mother was Ahab's daughter. Jehu's soldiers killed Jezebel and Ahaziah's forty-two relatives, Ahab's "great men" and relatives, and the priests of Baal. Jehu commanded Ahab's seventy sons to be killed by their guardians. As 2 Kings 10:10 reads, "Know now that there shall fall unto the earth nothing of the word of the Lord, which the Lord spake concerning the house of Ahab: for the Lord hath done *that* which he spake by his servant Elijah."

Following the account in Luke 9, the next chapter begins by saying,

> After these things the Lord appointed other seventy also and sent them two and two before his face into every city and place, whither he himself would come. Therefore said he unto them, The harvest truly *is* great, but the labourers

are few: pray ye therefore the Lord of the harvest, that he would send forth labourers into his harvest.

There was a definite reason why Jesus would send out seventy others beside his disciples. He came to receive our judgment, unlike the seventy sons of Ahab, who received the judgment due their father along with the rest of their family.

The irony in all this is that even though Jehu administered the judgment, he did not obey God's laws and was involved in the schismatic worship of both Yahweh and the golden calf. Unknowingly, James and John brought this story full circle and knowingly Jesus would lay his life down for all who deserve death because of sin. Jesus came to save lives, not to destroy them.

We have to understand James and John and their desire to defend Jesus. They wanted to stand up for Him, but that would have been a severe way to handle the rejection by the Samaritans. Have you ever tried to defend Jesus only to be unlike Him? If we meet people that won't receive Christ, do we try to defend Him or do we treat them in a Christ like manner? Jesus told us to bless those that curse us. Our greatest challenge is to love people into the kingdom of God as we labor in the harvest.

BAPTISM BY FIRE

I am come to send fire on the earth; and what will I if it be already kindled? But I have a baptism to be baptized with; and how am I straitened [distressed] till it be accomplished! (Luke 12:49–50)

It is my understanding that these verses definitely deal with a baptism by fire. Previously, in the section called Refined by Fire, Zechariah 13:8–9; I showed how Jesus explained that His crucifixion was the baptism He was distressed about. In Mark 10:35–45, James and John, the sons of Zebedee, asked Jesus if they could be beside Him in glory. My *Bible Dictionary* relates their father was a wealthy fisherman who had hired servants according to Mark 1:19–20. Perhaps this is why they considered themselves entitled to a place of honor. Jesus wondered if they could receive the same baptism and drink the same cup He was to receive. They responded, "we can" signifying their willingness to die for the Lord. Jesus said they would but wasn't able to promise the position they wanted. Jesus went on to tell them if they wanted to be great in the kingdom they would have to be a servant to all just as He did not come to be ministered to but to give His life as a "ransom for many."

Hebrews 13:10–12 draws the comparison that just as the bodies of the animals used in the sacrifices were burned outside the camp so was Jesus that "he might sanctify the people with his own blood, suffered without the gate." Spiritually, I see this referring to the Lord's crucifixion as His baptism by fire. I've also come to the conclusion that as we are to be living sacrifices we also receive that baptism by fire. As we come to the waters of baptism, our "old man" dies. As we submit to the baptism by fire, our "new man" dies. This is how we become servants.

In Luke 12:41–48 before Jesus talks about fire and baptism Peter is asking Jesus if He is speaking the previous parables in verses 35–40 to "us or even to all?" Once again, the Lord talks about servants before and after this question. Servants are warned to be prepared, waiting for the Lord's return, "faithful and wise" stewards doing their master's will. Those who abuse their position will be treated as unbelievers. Those who knew their master's will but didn't do it will receive a greater punishment than those who didn't know. After the verses about fire and baptism, Jesus explains that He has come to bring division rather than peace in families. He also called those who discern the weather but not the signs of the times hypocrites. The chapter ends with the Lord encouraging those who are being taken before authorities to attempt to reconcile with their adversary or pay all that they own.

Since the Lord surrounds this message of baptism and fire with warnings to be ready by discerning the times as faithful servants, we who are living in these last days understand how serving Him can bring division instead of peace. We will continually be challenged to die to ourselves in serving Him. As born again believers, we can walk in the power of the baptism of the Holy Spirit. If we are willing to be baptized by His Holy Fire, we can "know him in the power of his resurrection, and the fellowship of his sufferings, being made conformable unto his death," as written in Philippians 4:10. There could be no greater intimacy in our relationship with the Lord Jesus Christ.

RAINING FIRE

> Likewise also as it was in the days of Lot; they did eat, they drank, they bought, they sold, they planted, they builded; But the same day that Lot went out of Sodom it rained fire and brimstone from heaven, and destroyed them all. Even thus shall it be in the day when the son of man is revealed. (Luke 17:28–30)

Jesus made reference to the story found in Genesis 18–19:29. Abraham entertained three men whom Abraham calls "My Lord." He and Sarah were given the promise of a son at that meeting in the plains of Mamre. When the two men left for Sodom, the Lord wondered if He should hide from Abraham what He was going to do there. Abraham must have known because he interceded with the Lord for the righteous. Two angels went to Lot, Abraham's nephew, and led him and his family away from the perverse city. After the two angels told Lot to escape to the mountains, in chapter 19 verse 18 we read, "And Lot said unto them, Oh, not so my Lord" because he wanted to go to a closer city because he was afraid he would die in the mountains.

Notice Lot calls them, "My Lord." Why are the angels then called "Lord" in the singular? In chapter 19 verse 13, we are told that the angels were told to destroy the city. In chapter 19 verse 24, we read, "then the Lord rained upon Sodom and Gomorrah brimstone and fire from the Lord out of heaven." In chapter 19 verse 29, it says that God destroyed the cities of the plain. Throughout chapter 19, the words "men" and "angels" are used interchangeably to refer to the two who visited Lot's house. Could this be an example of the Trinity personified in the Old Testament?

In Revelation 11:8, we are told before the two witnesses come back to life and are taken up to heaven during the tribulation they will be killed by the beast and lie for three and a half days in the streets of a place, which is spiritually called Sodom and Egypt and also where the Lord was crucified. Why would this place have three spiritual names? Perhaps the reason is because fire was present in all three locations. The two witnesses prophesied for three and a half years and were able to have fire come out of their mouth to kill anyone who would try to harm them. The Lord sent fire on Sodom and Gomorrah after the two angels rescued Lot and his family. Moses stretched out his rod and fire from the Lord came down on Egypt. In both cases, this was a judgment from the Lord. In the section called "The Baptism of Fire," I explained that the crucifixion of the Lord was the Lord receiving our judgment as He was spiritually burned as the sacrifice for our sins.

In Luke 17:20–21, the Pharisees demanded to know when the kingdom of God would come. Jesus told them it would not come by observation or by going to a place but it was within them. I believe He said this because they knew the written word. In the rest of the chapter when Jesus is speaking to His disciples, He told them even though they would desire to see *one* of the days of the Son of man, they would not be able to. Verses 24–25 reads, "For as the lightning, that lighteneth out of the one *part* under heaven, shineth unto the other *part* under heaven; so shall also the Son of man be in his day. But first must he suffer many things, and be rejected of this generation." Then Jesus compares that time to the way things were for Abraham and Lot. Life went on as usual in the midst of perversion before destruction came. Verse 30 reads, "Even thus shall it be in the day when the Son of man is revealed." So the coming of the kingdom of God and the coming of the Son of man, the day of the Son of man and the revelation of the Son of man are the same thing.

The two angels came to rescue the only righteous people from Sodom before it was destroyed. Moses delivered God's people from their bondage in Egypt. The two witnesses will come to prophesy to those on the earth before the Lord pours out His wrath. In Matthew 24, when the disciples asked Jesus what would be the sign of His coming and of the end of the world, we learn the Lord said He will send His angels to gather His elect before the coming of the "Son of man."

14

JOHN

Abide in me, and I in you. As the branch cannot bear fruit of itself, except it abide in the vine; no more can ye, except ye abide in me. I am the vine, ye *are* the branches: He that abideth in me, and I in him, the same bringeth forth much fruit: for without me ye can do nothing. If a man abide not in me, he is cast forth as a branch, and is withered: and men gather them, and cast *them* into the fire and they are burned. If ye abide in me, and my words abide in you, ye shall ask what ye will, and it shall be done unto you. Herein is my Father glorified, that ye bear much fruit; so shall ye be my disciples. (John 15:4–8)

This chapter begins with Jesus telling his disciples that He is the true vine and the Father is the husbandman, the one who tends to the vineyard. Second Timothy 2:6 tells us that the husbandman is the first partaker of the fruits. By abiding in the vine, we will bear much fruit, which means we will bring many to the saving knowledge of Jesus Christ so that they might also be part of the vine.

In verse 2, we learn that the fruitless branches are taken away and the fruitful branches are pruned in order to produce more fruit. If you cut back a branch, usually that single branch will then become two. As the pruning continues, the branches multiply exponentially. The end result is there are more branches to produce more fruit. Figuratively, the Lord is referring to how we are able to help others along in the faith by going through this process at the Father's hand.

Verse 3 would seem out of context of we didn't consider that in the Old English Version the word "purgeth" is used instead of pruned. The modern concept of the word purge is to empty and so it is as branches of the true vine we will be emptied of ourselves so the life of Jesus will flow through us. Jesus said, "Now ye are clean through the word which I have spoken unto you." So the principle of abiding requires that we regularly spend time studying the word of God.

Just as the prophets spoke to God's people in this passage, Jesus is speaking to His own. There are only two kinds of branches: those who are alive and fruitful or those who are withered and fruitless. How is it possible to be part of the body of Christ and be withered? I can visualize a broken branch as one that is not drawing enough nourishment from the main plant. This could be compared to not spending time in fellowship with the Lord. In Matthew 25:41, Jesus tells those to depart from Him because He never knew them. It's one thing to know Him but only through time with Him will we be sure that He knows us.

How tragic when one chooses to remain withered and the end is to be taken away and gathered by men to be burned by fire. The part of that phrase "taken away" shows that, by not abiding in Christ, we could be separated from those who are abiding and the other part, "gathered by men" seems to imply that we are influenced by those outside the church. So why are the men doing the "burning by fire?" Could it be that the Lord would allow those who choose not to abide to experience a spiritual torment here in order to prevent them from the eternal torment in the hereafter?

I must confess that I have experienced both being alive and being withered. The times that I am disciplined in study, prayer, and worship I enjoy what John 15:11 says, "These things have I spoken unto you, that my joy might remain in you, and *that* your joy might be full." Other times, when I start to watch too much TV or sleep too much and miss my quiet time with the Lord, I notice the absence of that joy. It was David that wrote in Psalm 16:11…in his presence is fullness of joy.

However, let me be transparent about the purging process while I was being fruitful. I don't like it. I once heard the chorus of a song that expresses my attitude, "This dying to myself is killing me." I was going through one of those empty times and complaining to the Lord how I didn't think He ever went through what I was going through. The Holy Spirit convicted me when He reminded me of when Isaiah prophesied of the Lord's crucifixion where in part of chapter 53 verse 12 he said… because he hath poured out his soul unto death. Now I realize that being purged-emptied-poured out is all part of the process as we continue to share in the "fellowship of His suffering" as found in Philippians 3:10, while we are "being made conformable unto his death." Through it all, we will be able to "know him and the power of his resurrection." That is why Jesus said, "Apart from me you can do nothing."

I thought I had finished this section when one day the Lord led me back to this chapter and I noticed that chapter 16 seems to be a continuation of 15. Of course, when this gospel was first written, there were no separations in the text. First, consider this overview of what Jesus taught in John 15: We are to abide in Him, in His word and in His love; we will be fruitful and our fruit will remain; our joy will be full; Jesus calls us His friends; the world will hate and persecute us; the Comforter will come Who is the Spirit of truth; the Holy Spirit will testify of Jesus and bear witness of Him.

The first verse of John 16 reads, "These things have I spoken unto you, that ye should not be offended." I was curious what the word offended meant in the Greek so I looked it up in my *Key Word Study Bible*. One of the definitions was apostasy. I should not have been surprised since it seems that Jesus is speaking not only to the times that would come upon the disciples but also to the end times church. Chapter 16 ends with, "These things I have spoken unto you that in me ye might have peace. In the world ye shall have tribulation; but be of good cheer I have overcome the world." Jesus is warning of the persecution to come and how the Holy Spirit will help by leading us in all truth. He uses the analogy of a woman in the pain of childbirth to compare how our sorrow will be turned to joy in chapter 16 verses 20–21. In Matthew, the reference to the times of tribulation is called the beginning of sorrows. The Lord knew of the apostasy that would come as a result of the times of testing so He tells the disciples and the believers who will go through part of the tribulation how to endure. We must abide in Him. We must abide in His love. We must abide in His word.

15

ACTS

TONGUES OF FIRE

And when the day of Pentecost was fully come, they were all with one accord in one place. And suddenly there came a sound from heaven as of a rushing mighty wind, and it filled all the house where they were sitting. And there appeared unto them cloven tongues like as of fire, and it sat upon each of them. And they were all filled with the Holy Ghost, and began to speak with other tongues, as the Spirit gave them utterance. (Acts 2:1–4)

In an effort to learn more about the gift of speaking in tongues, I started by looking up each word in my *Key Word Study Bible*. Then I looked up online each word's definition in the Greek. Biblos.com is an easy way to learn the definition of each word in the above verses using *Strong's Concordance* of the King James Version. I also read some commentaries and even searched the Internet. I was surprised to find out that scientific research has been done to study the brain while someone is speaking in tongues. Finally, in my *Bible Dictionary*, I read of opposing viewpoints regarding Paul's discourse on the gifts of tongues and of prophecy in 1 Corinthians 14 versus the impartation in Acts 2. Personal experience has shown me that there is variety of opinions regarding this gift from the Holy Spirit.

It is unfortunate that in some churches, leaders would have everyone believe they should have this gift as if it were some sign of being more spiritual. To my dismay, I have heard prayers demanding the gift. It's not a gift if you have to beg for it. The Holy Spirit moves as He wills. Some churches allow those who have the gift to speak openly without interpretation and some do not. I have the gift and I never asked for it.

I was three years into my walk with the Lord when I was listening to a song by Leon Patillo. He sang, "Listen to the voice." I didn't know then he was speaking about the still small voice that Elijah heard. He also sang the names of the Lord: Yahweh and Elohim. I was sitting in my car in my driveway listening to the tape. When I got out of my car and sat on the porch swing, I began speaking in tongues. I asked the Lord to interpret it and He graciously did. I used to try to write it down so I wouldn't forget it. It was such an incredible experience. I am naturally attracted to different languages because my father and mother spoke English, Spanish, French, and German. I do fairly well with Spanish and I was surprised how much I understood the first time I visited my relatives in France. My spiritual language has grown and sometimes I understand what I am saying. It is both humbling and encouraging to speak in tongues.

If we simply look at the text in the first verse, we learn it was given on the day of Pentecost. This Jewish festival was celebrated on the fiftieth day after Passover. Jesus sacrificed His life for us on Passover. The most significant detail to me is they were in one place and were of one accord. We read that same thing in Acts 1:14. Truly, when God's people are of one accord…He moves.

An Old Testament example of this is when the people praised God with one voice as Solomon dedicated the temple and the glory of God was so strong no one could stand up. A summary of Zephaniah 3 shows the Lord is in our midst to sing and rejoice over us after we've been afflicted, corrected and if we walk in unity and purity. I pray for this kind of unity that would allow us to experience the Lord's presence.

Some believe the gift of tongues ceased after the first believers died and no longer exists. Others believe the gift was revived during the Pentecostal Movement of the early 1900s and is still given. My *Bible Dictionary* mentions Irenaeus, sixty years after the last apostle died, aware of "many brethren who had prophetic gifts and spoke through the Spirit in all kinds of tongues." It also records in 1830 and 1831, there were those in Scotland and London who demonstrated the gifts. I've also heard that the gift of speaking in tongues never ceased but rather was suppressed by church officials.

The Greek language reveals some interesting things about this passage. Notice it is a "sound" like a rushing mighty wind. This word for wind *pneo* comes from a word that means to "breathe hard" and is the root word for *pneuma* which is Greek for Holy Ghost. The word *cloven* means to "partition thoroughly in distribution." The word for *tongue* in the Greek is "glossa" and by combining it with *lalia* which means to articulate words, "glossalalia" becomes a seldom-used word that means speaking in tongues. In Mark 16:17, the phrase "speak with new tongues" is rendered "laleo glossais." *Laleo* in the Greek is used when it says that God "spake in times past" in Hebrews 1:1–2. So essentially, the breath of the Holy Spirit was equally distributed among those in the upper room and He gave them a new language. In Genesis, on the first day, God spoke and there was light. The word for light could have been translated fire. Also, when God breathed the "breath of life" into Adam, the ancient Hebrew manuscripts translate "man became a living soul" as "man became a living fire." Those in the upper room were baptized by the fire of His breath and spoke as the Holy Spirit "gave them utterance," as Jesus promised they would receive "power from on high."

Could it be the breath of fire was restored on the first Pentecost? Imagine the two witnesses in Revelation 11 who are able to destroy their enemies with fire from their mouths. The sword of the Spirit is the word of God. For those of us who believe in the gift of tongues and use it appropriately, we have no idea the spiritual warfare that is accomplished through its declarations by the power of the Holy Spirit!

PAUL BUILDS A FIRE

And when they were escaped, then they knew that the island was called Melita. And the barbarous people shewed us no little kindness: for they kindled a fire, and received us everyone, because of the present rains, and because of the cold. And when Paul had gathered a bundle of sticks, and laid *them* on the fire, there came a viper out of the heat, and fastened on his hand. And when the barbarians saw the *venomous* beast hang on his hand, they said among themselves, No doubt this man is a murderer, who though he hath escaped the sea, yet vengeance suffereth not to live. And he shook off the beast into the fire, and felt no harm. Howbeit they looked when he should have swollen, or fallen down dead suddenly: but after they had looked a great while, and saw no harm come to him, they changed their minds, and said that he was a god. (Acts 28:1–6)

As believers who want to be used by God in a mighty way, we need to look at the testimony of Paul's life. When the Lord first appeared to Paul, He told him that he would suffer many things for Him. Imagine if churches today called repentant sinners into a relationship with Jesus this way? Paul's conversion was so profound that he willingly did so. In 2 Corinthians 12:10, he says, "Therefore I take pleasure in infirmities, in reproaches, in necessities, in persecutions, in distresses for Christ's sake: for when I am weak, then am I strong." In chapter 13 verse 4, he continues, "For though he [Jesus] was crucified through weakness, yet he liveth by the power of God. For we also are weak in him, but we shall live with him by the power of God toward you."

In the surrounding chapters of the verse we are considering, Paul was being sent by God to preach in Rome as a prisoner. How does that sound as a speaking engagement? Against Paul's warning on board that the vessel could be lost, the ship owners decided to sail and found themselves facing rough seas. An "angel of God" appeared to Paul saying, "Fear not, Paul: thou must be brought before Caesar; and, *lo*, God hath given thee all them that sail with thee." Paul lets those onboard know it would be as the angel promised but they would be "cast upon a certain island." It was imperative that they stay on the ship to stay alive. So Paul encouraged them to eat meat, break bread, and blessed it following a fourteen-day fast. Even when all end up alive on shore after the shipwreck, the soldiers onboard wanted to kill Paul and all the prisoners but were stopped by the centurion. This is how they ended up on this island also known as Malta being treated kindly by the "barbarians."

Do we recognize the providential hand of the Lord in all circumstances? None of this happened by chance. It was ordained of God that Paul should heal those with diseases on this island. It was purposed that a viper would come out of the heat and attached itself to Paul's hand. I can't help but wonder why, Luke, the author of this narrative would change his description of the snake to a "*venomous* beast." I have learned that everything means something in the Bible. It seems this word in the Greek has its roots in a word that also means destruction or trap. So often I have seen God move after great trials. Paul knew his ultimate destination and purpose. He merely shook it off. Wouldn't it be great if we could just shake off the opposition we encounter when we decide to serve God? Maybe we can, if we are walking in the kind of faith that only the Lord can give us. This is why Paul admonished the Corinthians to, "Examine yourselves, whether ye be in the faith; prove your own selves. Know ye not your own selves, how that Jesus Christ be in you, except you be reprobates?" There is so much "soft-selling" in some churches today. Are we really being challenged to deny ourselves, take up our cross, and follow Jesus? How did we get to this place? Has our culture of comfort invaded our fellowships? The chairs have to be cushioned, the air-conditioning has to be at the right temperature, and whatever happens, do not let the service go on too long.

Furthermore, while in their minds, the barbarians thought Paul was a god, we don't read anywhere in this account that he tried to change their thinking by correcting them. I think of missionaries that stripped ethnic people of their cultural identity. Neither was he offended when they considered him a murderer and deserved "vengeance." Instead, he healed their diseases. When Paul spoke to the pagans in Rome, he explained to them who their unknown god was by telling them about Jesus. Jesus doesn't focus on the externals but the heart. He hung out with sinners; they were attracted to Him. Some churches tend to repel sinners with their lack of grace and list of rules. The Holy Spirit is the one who changes people's hearts and behavior, not us. Loving people should be our first priority. Trusting God through any trial will be our proving ground. Accepting that there will be obstacles and hindrances is our challenge. Seeing God move on our behalf will be our testimony.

16

1 CORINTHIANS

REVEALED BY FIRE

Every man's work shall be made manifest: for the day shall declare it, because it shall be revealed by fire; and the fire shall try every man's work of what sort it is. If any man's work abide which he hath built thereupon, he shall receive a reward. If any man's work shall be burned, he shall suffer loss: but he himself shall be saved; yet so as by fire. (1 Corinthians 3:13–15)

This chapter begins with Paul telling the Corinthian Christians he needed to address them as carnal and juvenile for their divisions and strife. Apparently, there were contentions regarding whose teachings the believers adhered to, whether it was Paul or Apollos, based on who brought them to faith. Paul explains that the ones who plant or water for the harvest are nothing, but it is God that "gives the increase" and so it is we are to labor together because we are "God's building." With this, Paul claims to be a "wise masterbuilder" solely by God's grace and declares the only foundation that can be built upon is Jesus Christ. The gold, silver, precious stones, wood, hay or stubble are those teachings that are laid upon the foundation of Christ, who is the Word of God. The work Paul is describing is the work of expounding upon the scriptures.

Usually, the expression of our works being burned in the fire is taught to pertain to the things that we do as Christians. Those things that withstand the fire were done with the right motives. That's what I always thought until I looked closer at this chapter. Paul is warning all followers of Christ to "take heed" how they build upon that foundation. He wants the readers of this letter to know there can be no other foundation laid except that of Jesus Christ. This grave admonition goes to all who would teach the Word of God.

The choice of words in verse 13 is intriguing. The word *manifest* in the Greek is "phaneros," a conjugation of the word "phaino." and has its roots in the word for fire or light. That root word is *phos* and its definition is "to make manifest especially by rays." Another word *phemi* has the same base as phos and phaino and means "to make known one's thoughts."

Paul goes on to explain the "day shall declare it." Just as in 1 Corinthians 4:5, we read, "Therefore judge nothing before the time until the Lord come, who both will bring to light the hidden things of darkness and will make manifest the counsels of the hearts and then shall every man have praise of God." How are we to understand "that day?"

Once, I did a study of Genesis in the Hebrew. In researching the words found in Genesis 1, I came to the conclusion that when the Lord said let there be light and evening and morning were the first day, essentially it translates, in my own words, to mean God covers and uncovers the light. After all, the sun and moon were not created until the fourth day. The word for light in the Hebrew could have also been translated fire. (See the Introduction to this book). On this day, the works will be revealed by fire. The word for reveal in the Greek is number 601 and is the basis for the word apocalypse. This word also means to "uncover."

Imagine for a moment the new heaven and new earth as spoken of in the last two chapters of Revelation. There is no need of a sun or moon because the glory of the Lord is there. Since our God is a "consuming fire," just the presence of the Lord is the fire that will reveal the purity of those works. Those who taught the word will either "receive a reward" or "suffer loss." Verse 15 explains that those whose works are burned up will be saved "as if by fire."

The remainder of the chapter addresses the reality of believers being the temple of God. The warning goes out to not defile the temple because God's temple is holy. This impacts me heavily with the weight of responsibility while working on this book. Our work and personal purity are closely related. Sometimes works are placed over holiness and I believe that is why ministries fail. By not building on Christ as the foundation and being wise in our own eyes and then allowing sin to enter in to our hearts, minds or body, our work in the kingdom is doomed.

Paul also tells us not to be deceived by anyone who claims to be "wise in this world" because it is foolishness to God and He knows it is vanity. How relevant is verse 21 today: Therefore let no man glory in men? Do you worry as I do about the cult of personalities that have invaded pulpits across America? Are we following a teacher or following Jesus? Paul's answer is, "Ye are Christ's; and Christ's is God." Let a man so account of us, as of the ministers of Christ, and stewards of the mysteries of God. What greater privilege or responsibility could there be?

17

2 THESSALONIANS

A FLAMING FIRE TAKING VENGEANCE

And to you who are troubled rest with us, when the Lord Jesus shall be revealed from heaven with his mighty angels, In flaming fire taking vengeance on them that know not God, and that obey not the gospel of our Lord Jesus Christ: Who shall be punished with everlasting destruction from the presence of the Lord, and from the glory of his power; When he shall come to be glorified in his saints, and to be admired in all them that believe (because our testimony among you was believed) in that day. (2 Thessalonians 1:7–10)

Paul wrote to the early Christians in Thessalonica to encourage them despite the suffering they endured because of intense persecution. Paul claims in the fifth verse of the first chapter that this tribulation is a "manifest token of the righteous judgment of God," and commends them as being "counted worthy of the kingdom of God," for which they suffered. The vengeance, punishment, and destruction to come is "a righteous thing with God" and will be administered to "recompense tribulation" to all those who "troubled" these believers according to verse 6. They are told to "rest" with Paul and the other believers in this knowledge.

"In that day," the Lord will be "revealed from heaven with His mighty angels" in a "flaming fire." Once again, the word used for reveal in the Greek implies to "take off the cover." Here we could apply the imagery of the heavens rolled up, as if they were a scroll, as written of in both Isaiah 34:4 and Revelation 6:14.

Isaiah's graphic depiction of this destruction is the "day of the Lord's vengeance, and the year of recompense for the controversy of Zion," according to chapter 34 verse 8. The devastation turns the land into burning pitch and smoking brimstone. John, the Revelator, places this event at the opening of the sixth seal when the sun is blackened and the moon looks blood red. The mountains and islands are moved out of place and men cry out for the rocks to fall on them to hide them from "the wrath of the Lamb." John writes, "For the great day of his wrath is come; and who shall be able to stand?" I maintain those who are able to stand are those who have been tried/baptized by His holy fire.

Only the uncovering of the holy fire of God could make the radiance of the sun disappear. Paul used the phrase "flaming fire" for double emphasis to give the intensity of the Lord's appearance. The root word for flaming in the Greek is *phlox* and means to "flash or flame like a blaze." Remember, Matthew 24 tells us that after the sun and moon are darkened and the stars fall and the heavens are shook, then "the sign of the Son of man in heaven" shall appear. This sign would have to be that flaming fire because Matthew goes on to let us know that all the tribes of the earth will mourn at this appearance. Then the angels will go to gather the elect from the "four winds and from one end of heaven to the other." Those who did not know God or rejected the gospel of Jesus Christ are doomed. The destruction is one thing, but to be eternally separated from God and from the glory of His power is in my opinion the worst consequence of all.

How could a loving God allow this kind of retribution to take place? It is because those who rejected Jesus decided not to take the greatest plea bargain ever made…that He would take their punishment at the cross. God, the Father made a way of escape from this wrath. He gave us Jesus, His only Son, to be put to death for our sins so we could have eternal life. Jesus took the punishment for all. Justice demands punishment. Even though "mercy rejoices against judgment," if someone is unwilling to receive the benefits of that mercy, they have sentenced themselves.

As believers, we know and understand the wrath of God, when we hear the Lord say that vengeance belongs to Him. To know the fear of God is the beginning of knowledge and wisdom. Without the fear of God, there is no understanding. In Revelation, we hear how the saints in heaven cry out to God asking how much longer until He avenges the blood of the prophets. Retribution is the natural consequence of rebellion. We are either with God or against Him. Who among us cannot understand justice? Our holy God judges righteously.

The only thing God will not interfere with is our freewill. The One, who has the power to make the heavens depart, whose glory is from everlasting to everlasting, whose eternal fire burns with a passionate love for us, has given us the power to refuse Him or accept Him. As the writer of Hebrews says, today if you will hear His voice do not harden your heart. To know Him, the Great I AM and to obey the gospel of Jesus is the privilege of all who chose to accept the gift of eternal life.

18

HEBREWS

And of the angels he saith, Who maketh his angels spirits, and his ministers a flame of fire…Are they not all ministering spirits, sent forth to minister for them who shall be heirs of salvation? (Hebrews 1:7, 14)

I write to testify of how the Lord has sent His angels to minister to me. Most of the time, we are unaware of the work they are doing on our behalf. Angels are also called Seraphim and Cherubim. I believe this text is talking about Seraphim because the word in the Hebrew translates as "burning ones."

The first time I was aware that angels were ministering to me was after I had a miscarriage. I believe they ushered me in the spirit to see the smiling blue eyes of the baby girl I had lost to heaven. The next time I was aware of their presence was after my husband, John, had a stroke and he had to learn to walk again. After months of rehabilitation, I watched him from our home on a hill as he made his way around the block. There were angels on both sides of him.

I saw angels standing at the head of the bed of a godly woman dying of cancer. I found myself weeping not for her or her family or even from my reaction to the sadness but from a grief I couldn't explain. I left the hospital that night and prayed for the Lord to help me understand. He simply spoke, "They will not release her to Me." The next day at the hospital, we saw her husband first and I told him about the angels and what the Lord had said. I had brought oil to anoint her body, which he immediately took and privately released her to the Lord. These events prepared me for the most intense ministry of angels I have ever experienced.

On August 4, 2009, our son Billy, gave his dad one of his kidneys. While they were both in recovery from a successful transplant operation, John had a heart attack. Five hours later, we learned that he was on life support and they wanted permission to use a dye that could damage the transplanted kidney and to give him blood transfusions. For the next two hours, my daughters, Kimberly and Crystal, and son Johnny kept a vigil of praying, reading our granddaughter's Bible and praising God. Billy was ministering the word to his wife, Brynne, while he was in the hospital room recovering. Our son Tommy and his wife, Danielle, in Chicago joined us in spirit, but were ready to leave that night to drive to Tucson with their newborn, Brave Daniel. Kim's husband Bill and his family had just learned his sister had been sent home in the final stages of cancer and he was at his home with their daughter Giavella praying. Cory, Crystal's husband, was at home praying with their children Makenna and Mason. I could only call immediate family for prayer. Everyone started a prayer chain through text messages.

As much as the Lord had brought us through, I knew I needed to trust Him and we prayed for His will. I have always resorted to praising the Lord in times of trouble because it resets my focus on the Lord and because it confuses the enemy. The doctors at the Mayo Clinic did not give us much hope, but when they let us see John, I put my hand on his heart and prayed out loud in tongues. At one point, all we could do was hold on to each other and cry. I was so overwhelmed I thought I was going to pass out, but after splashing some water on my face, I knew this is what the Lord had been preparing me for in the preceding months before the transplant operation.

We had sold our home and had to build a garage to store our belongings in while we were living in our Airstream on some land near the Saguaro National Park. I had started listening to a prophetic worship music station online called Elijah Streams. One day, I heard a song that had native Indian style percussion. I ordered two albums from Cheryl Bear and that's all I listened to while I helped John build our garage. All the songs are so anointed but one in particular stayed in my heart. Some of the words to the chorus are: Rise up new warrior, Jesus is our Greatest Chief, He will give the victory against our enemy, My spear is the word of God and my shield is the shield of faith. I am ready to take my stand. This would be my theme song for the next ten days.

It wasn't until after midnight that the doctors said they were able to put four new stents in his heart to open up the blocked vessels. He also was given seven units of blood which was a full blood transfusion. We were so relieved but had no idea at that time the battle that was set before us. John was on a breathing pump and a heart pump and was heavily sedated to give his heart a chance to heal. It gave me a couple of days to eat, rest, and pray. When they began to wean him off the sedatives, he was very agitated and confused. I told the nurses to just say that our son Billy was all right. We knew that was his main concern. One morning, Crystal read a verse of promise from Psalm 91:14–16 that says,

Because he hath set his love upon me, therefore will I deliver him: I will set him on high, because he hath known my name. He shall call upon me, and I will answer him: I *will be* with him in trouble; I will deliver him and honour him. With long life will I satisfy him and shew him my salvation.

Once they removed the breathing tube from his throat, John kept saying, "Light this match and hold it up high, I can't see, it's dark." At night, I would go back to my daughter, Kim's house and pray, "Lord, help me understand what he's going through." The Lord showed me a dark corridor. It reminded me of a song on Cheryl Bear's CD of the struggle we all will face as we pass from this life to the next. When they got John off the heart pump, he looked like a child crying and he was asking for his mother and father.

I knew there was a spiritual battle going on for his life. I wanted to meditate on Psalm 91 and hide in the "secret place of the Most High and in the shadow of his wings," but the Lord took me to Hebrews 1 and said, "Pray against any hindrance to the ministry of my angels." It reminded me of how Daniel had fasted and prayed for twenty-one days while the enemy withstood the Lord before Michael came to help Daniel understand the visions for the end times found in Chapter 10. So I began to take my stand as a "new warrior" on John's behalf. In the morning, when I got to the hospital, I could spiritually see the angels around his bed. There was a calm bright presence that overtook his room where previously there had been darkness and chaos.

John and I had both experienced drug trips during the seventies, and since they used narcotics to keep him sedated, I knew this is where the battle was going on. Drugs are the devil's playground even though I understood the need for them. After three days, John was in what I call a loop…the nurses could not handle his aggressive behavior so they would continue to sedate him. I went outside and called a friend of mine, Pat Lutz, to pray because of her keen insight in this realm due to her many years of intercessory prayer and ministry to women in jail and to those coming off of drugs. She powerfully covered this situation with the precious blood of Jesus and took rightful authority over the situation. It was amazing what happened after that prayer. The Lord sent a tall strong nurse who stood like Mr. Clean and assertively spoke a definitive plan to get John off the narcotics. Through the night, I called every few hours and was assured all was well. Even though I knew it, I had to ask the nurse if he was a Christian. He boldly answered, "Oh, yes I am!" When I got to the hospital, John's demeanor had changed even though he was still coming off the drugs. At one point, while sitting up, he pointed down the hall and shouted, "Look, it's a wedding and everyone is invited." The following morning, I asked the Lord to show me what John was seeing. In the spirit, I saw an arm grab my arm to lift me up to where I saw a beautiful angel standing at a doorway to a large peaceful expanse of opaque bright light. I knew it was a room where the souls of believers are. I knew that John had been between here and eternity and the Lord wasn't through counting the "number of his days."

We spent seven weeks after John was released from the hospital going for follow-up doctor visits, blood test, and cardio rehabilitation. We spent many days in the hospital cafeteria where nurses and doctors would come up to John and say, "It's amazing how good you look." Even those who weren't believers acknowledged that it was a miracle. Psalm 104:4 declares of God that He makes His angels spirits; His ministers a flaming fire. May we as heirs to salvation, because of our faith in Jesus Christ, who Himself was ministered to by angels at His temptation and before He was crucified, all experience that ministry of angels who are like flames of fire.

And what shall I more say? For the time would fail me to tell of Gedeon, and *of* Barak, and *of* Samson, and *of* Jephthae; *of* David also, and Samuel, and *of the* prophets: Who through faith subdued kingdoms, wrought righteousness, obtained promises, stopped the mouths of lions, quenched the violence of fire, escaped the edge of the sword, out of weakness were made strong, waxed valiant in fight, turned to flight the armies of the aliens. (Hebrews 11:33–34)

This chapter begins with the most incredible description of faith: "Now faith is the substance of things hoped for, the evidence of things not seen." The writer delivers a brief overview of the history of some of the Bible's greatest heroes describing what they accomplished as a result of their faith in God. Verse 13 reads, "These all died in faith, not having received the promises, but having seen them afar off, and were persuaded of *them*, and embraced *them*, and confessed that they were strangers and pilgrims on the earth." They were convinced God was preparing a heavenly city for them.

By contrast, do we as believers, who have received the promise through faith in Jesus, have that intensity of anticipation? Enoch never died but was "translated" because he pleased God. Verse 6 says, "But without faith *it is* impossible to please *him*; for he that cometh to God must believe that he is, and *that* he is a rewarder of them that diligently seek him."

Apparently, there wasn't enough time for the writer to tell all the stories he had in mind but he did mention a few names. Some are more familiar than others, but he included the prophets as those whose faith had been tried. It is hard to comprehend how these heroes of faith could endure the sufferings mentioned in verses 35–38. Some women saw their dead brought back to life while others saw their loved ones tortured believing they would be delivered by a better resurrection. They were mocked and scourged, bound, and imprisoned. Some were stoned, cut in half, tempted, killed by the sword. They "wandered about in sheepskins and goatskin; being destitute, afflicted, tormented; (Of whom the world was not worthy:) they wandered in deserts, and *in* mountains, and *in* dens and caves of the earth." This is so far removed from how potential converts are enticed to enter into faith in some Christian churches today.

Chapter 11 was written to establish the first thoughts in chapter 12:

> Wherefore seeing we also are compassed about with so great a cloud of witnesses, let us lay aside every weight, and the sin which doth *so* easily beset *us,* and let us run with patience the race that is set before us, looking unto Jesus the author and finisher of *our* faith; who for the joy that was set before him endured the cross, despising the shame, and is set down at the right hand of the throne of God.

We are not to be "wearied and faint" in our minds because we have not yet "resisted unto blood striving against sin." What a precious price was paid for the promises delivered at the cross. The awareness of the "great cloud of witnesses," those who fought the good fight of faith, should encourage us to press on despite the trials we face. Jesus, knowing that we would be with Him in eternity, was able to endure the cross for us. Likewise, we should have the same mentality.

The time will come when those who are alive must deny Christ or die. There exists today the seed of that one world religious system that is tolerant of all faiths except the true Christian faith. There is also a diluted and polluted version of Christianity that follows the multitude of false prophets. Our dedication to the Word of God, our submission to the Holy One of Israel, our faith in the Triune God is all we will have should we be alive when the body of Christ is tested.

What is the basis of our faith? Was it an emotional response made to alleviate our suffering when in fact a walk of faith can be filled with suffering? Were we promised a life of peace and joy and happiness? Why do you think Jesus said that His peace was not like that found in the world? I believe many fall away from their faith because they are not willing to be tested and tried. From the first moment we make the decision to let Jesus be Lord of our lives, anything and everything will come against us to try to destroy our resolve. It would be better to know from the beginning so we would not be disillusioned when the struggles come.

Ephesians 6 tells us to take up the shield of faith, above all the other weapons, that we will be able to quench all the fiery darts of the wicked. The writer of Hebrews expressed a similar thought by saying those believers "quenched the violence of fire." We need to be ever mindful that we are in a battle. It is a battle for our souls and for the body of Christ. We are told to watch and occupy which are military terms. The church has let its guard down and consequently been assuaged by an infiltration of indulgence to self.

Church history has shown that many great revivals occurred as a result of persecution. I know that many missionaries face persecution and there are modern day martyrs, but the church in America has not yet experienced anything that would compare to what the first church faced. I believe that the final revival will not occur until the body of Christ in America endures persecution.

Once the Lord said to me, "A time of favor before the persecution, a time of persecution before the revival, a time of revival before the tribulation, a time of tribulation before the rapture." Daniel 7:25 and Revelation 13:7 both tell of a time when the saints of God will be overcome. The verse in Daniel specifically mentions the three-and-a-half-year period. May I be so bold as to say that the notion of a pre-tribulation rapture has lulled some churches to sleep in a foxhole while the battle rages on around her? I cry out for the Lord to have mercy, but in His sovereignty, He will allow a remnant to arise that will hold fast to the truth of His word and not be dissuaded from their faith.

MOUNTAIN BURNING WITH FIRE

For ye are not come unto the mount that might be touched, and that burned with fire, nor unto blackness, and darkness and tempest, And the sound of a trumpet, and the voice of words; which *voice* they that heard entreated that the word should not be spoken to them any more: (For they could not endure that which was commanded, And if so much as a beast touch the mountain, it shall be stoned, or thrust through with a dart: And so terrible was the sight that Moses said, I exceedingly fear and quake:) But you are come unto mount Sion, and unto the city of the living God, the heavenly Jerusalem, and to an innumerable company of angels, To the general assembly and church of the firstborn, which are written in heaven, and to God the Judge of all, and to the spirits of just men made perfect, And to Jesus the mediator of the new covenant, and to the blood of sprinkling, that speaketh better things than *that* of Abel. See that ye refuse not him that speaketh. For if they escaped not who refused him that spake on earth, much more *shall not* we *escape* if we turn away from him that *speaketh* from heaven. (Hebrews 12:18–25)

In this letter to the Hebrew Christians, the two mountains contrasted the benefits of the old covenant under the law with the new covenant under the blood of Jesus. Within the new covenant are rights given to those who have accepted this atonement. The privilege granted is to be able to enter into the presence of the Holy One of Israel. No longer do believers cower in physical fear from the fiery spectacle of a mountain that burned with the presence of God but rather bow in reverential fear to our God who is a consuming fire.

The mountain that burned with fire was Mount Sinai. After forty years, Moses saw "the angel of the Lord in a flame of fire in a bush" at mount Sina, as spelled in older translations of Acts 7:30. In this account, Stephen, before he was stoned to death, testified of the deliverance and rebellion of the Hebrews. Exodus 19 relates the events that preceded Moses receiving the Ten Commandments. Verse 18 says, "And mount Sinai was altogether on a smoke, because the Lord descended upon it in fire: and the smoke thereof ascended as the smoke of a furnace, and the whole mount quaked greatly." Those Hebrew that "stood at the nether part of the mount" were fearful of all the sights and sounds. There was thunder, lightning, thick darkness, and the voice of a trumpet that increased in volume. God had set a boundary "lest they break through unto the Lord to gaze, and many of them perish," according to verse 21.

Moses was the mediator who relayed God's desire found in verses 5–6: "Now therefore, if ye will obey my voice indeed, and keep my covenant, then ye shall be a peculiar treasure unto me above all people: for all the earth is mine: and ye shall be unto me a kingdom of priest, and an holy nation." The people replied, "all that the Lord hath spoken we will do." At the base of Mount Sinai, the covenant of law was ratified.

Mount Sinai was considered to be the mountain of God until the ark was moved to Jerusalem. Psalm 76:2 reads, "In Salem also is his tabernacle, and his dwelling place in Zion." In Genesis 14, Abram met Melchizedek the king of Salem, an abbreviation of Jerusalem, that meant "foundation of peace" or "secure habitation." According to my *Bible Dictionary*, the earliest version of this name was "Urusalim," found in an Egyptian text written before the sixteenth century BC. It was also referred to as Jebus, considered to be the aboriginal name. As a result, some thought the name of the holy city to be a contraction of Jebus and Salem.

The last syllable of the Hebrew word *Yruwshalain* was modified by the Jews to represent a "dual city" that has two hills.

Second Samuel 5:7 informed us it was a Jebusite fortress on a hill that David's army captured and called the city of David. "The ark of God whose name is called by the name of the Lord of hosts that dwelleth *between* the cherubims" was put in the "midst of the tabernacle that David had pitched for it," according to 2 Samuel 6:2 and 17. When the ark was moved to the temple, Solomon built on Mount Moriah, the word Zion was used to include the new temple. Zion is also used to refer to the Jewish church and those under its government. According to an online Hebrew Lexicon, it means monument, guiding pillar, sign, title, or waymark.

Isaiah 4:5 prophesied, "And the Lord will create upon every dwelling place of mount Zion, and upon her assemblies, a cloud and smoke by day, and the shining of a flaming fire by night; for upon all the glory *shall be* a defense." And there shall be a tabernacle for a shadow in the daytime from the heat, and for a place of refuge, and for a covert from storm and from rain. In chapter 24 verse 23, Isaiah also declared, after the whole earth is judged reeling to and fro like a drunkard, "Then the moon shall be confounded, and the sun ashamed, when the Lord of hosts shall reign in mount Zion, and in Jerusalem, and before his ancients gloriously." Joel 3:16 reads,

> The Lord also shall roar out of Zion, and utter his voice from Jerusalem; and the heavens and the earth shall shake: but the Lord *will be* the hope of his people, and the strength of the children of Israel. So shall ye know that I *am* the Lord your God dwelling in Zion, my holy mountain: then shall Jerusalem be holy, and there shall no strangers pass through her any more.

All of this information alludes to the millennial reign of Jesus.

In Hebrews and Revelation, the name for Zion is spelled Sion in older translations. The Greek word means "militant and triumphant" according to an online Greek Lexicon. It is not to be confused when used in the Old Testament to refer to Hermon in Deuteronomy 4:48.

In Revelation 14, John saw the Lamb that stood on mount Sion with the 144,000 that had "his Father's name written in their foreheads." We read of them being sealed in the seventh chapter of the same book. In Hebrews 12:22, we are told that Sion is "the city of the living God, the heavenly Jerusalem." How does all this information pertain to us, right here, right now?

My Bible Dictionary reveals the Ark of the Covenant or Testimony was considered the "centerpiece of the tabernacle." The wooden box, that held the tables of stone on which the Ten Commandments were written, was overlaid with gold. It had two golden cherubim facing each other with wings spread to cover the lid of the ark that looked down at the mercy seat. It was put in the Holy of Holies. In the Old Testament, it was symbolic of Jehovah's unapproachable presence. There He met and spoke with the representatives of the people. The Ark of the Covenant went before the people when leaving Sinai, went before them crossing the Jordan, was carried in the procession around Jericho, was removed to Shiloh, and captured by the Philistines. The people who viewed the inside of it were punished at Bethshemesh. Uzzah was struck dead when he touched it on the way back to Jerusalem, it briefly stayed in the house of Obed-edom, was then placed in Solomon's temple, but the Ark disappeared when Nebuchadnezzar destroyed Jerusalem.

Jeremiah prophesied of the new covenant that would be established in chapter 31 verses 31–33:

> Behold, the days come, saith the Lord, that I will make a
> new covenant with the house of Israel, and with house of
> Judah: Not according to the covenant that I made with
> their fathers in the day *that* I took them by the hand to

bring them out of the land of Egypt; which my covenant they brake, although I was an husband unto them, saith the Lord: But this *shall be* the covenant that I will make with the house of Israel; After those days, saith the Lord, I will put my laws in their inward parts, and write it in their heart; and I will be their God, and they shall be my people.

Hebrews 8 repeats this verse in the explanation of the need for the new covenant because according to verse 7, "For if that first *covenant* had been faultless, then should no place have been sought for the second." It is Jesus, our high priest, who "is set on the right hand of the throne of the Majesty in heavens; a minister of the sanctuary, and of the true tabernacle, which the Lord pitched and not man. It is our heart that becomes the Ark of the New Covenant, our bodies that become His temple. Spiritually, we are part of the general assembly, the church of the firstborn because our names are written in heaven. We can come before the Judge of all because Jesus has perfected us forever by His blood that was shed on the cross.

As believers, we are grafted into the vine, which is Israel. However, Jeremiah 31 is a promise for the future restoration of Zion as the Lord draws the "families of Israel" with "lovingkindness." His promise comes with the proviso that if the ordinances of the moon and stars would depart, then the seed of Israel would cease from being a nation. The prophecy ends with a description of dead bodies and ashes that cover a valley next to the Kidron Valley that becomes holy to the Lord. Would these ashes come as a result of His holy fire? Could it be this is what is meant by the verse in Hebrews 10:13 that describes the expected time when the Lord's enemies become His footstool?

We come to mount Sion to enter the heavenly Jerusalem, the city of the living God by the Holy Spirit of Jesus whose flesh was the torn veil that gave us access into the holy of holies. His laws written in our hearts ratifies the new covenant sealed with His precious blood. Jesus, as Messiah, will come to gather His people Israel to once again be their husband. Jerusalem will come down from heaven as His bride. In the Jewish tradition, the proposal of marriage was accepted upon drinking the cup of wine. Jesus said this cup is my blood of the new covenant in Matthew 26:27–28. Have you accepted His proposal? See to it that you don't refuse Him who speaks from heaven.

OUR GOD IS A CONSUMING FIRE

> Wherefore we receiving a kingdom which cannot be moved, let us have grace, whereby we may serve God acceptably with reverence and godly fear: For our God is a consuming fire. (Hebrews 12:28–29)

The prophet Haggai is quoted in the verses that precede the ones we are studying when we are told that "once more" there will be a shaking caused by the voice that once shook the earth but will also shake heaven. This shaking will prove what will stand and what will be removed. However, the kingdom that the Lord established cannot be moved. Jesus said His kingdom was not of this world. By our submission to His will for our lives, His kingdom is established in our hearts through the Holy Spirit. We need grace in order to serve Him in the proper way and we can only know how to have grace if we have received that grace.

We can hardly fathom with our natural mind the intensity of the words that describe God as a "consuming fire." We must have our understanding enlightened by the power of Holy Spirit. If God is a consuming fire and God is a Spirit, then logic would tell us that His Holy Spirit is fire. After all, His Spirit descended on the apostles in the upper room in what appeared as tongues of fire. When we read of the Lord being a pillar of fire to the Hebrews in the wilderness, I believe it was the consuming fire of

His Spirit. So why do we not have that awareness of His presence as a consuming fire unless we see it in a vision?

When Jesus spoke, He often said that there would be those who would see but not see. Jesus said He would never leave us or forsake us, but we are not always aware of His presence. We are guaranteed the Holy Spirit when we receive Jesus as Lord and Savior, but we so often drift back into our carnal ways. Would that we could be continually sensitive and aware of that holy consuming fire of God. How different would every moment of every day be? Do you believe it is possible? I do! Am I? No. Why? Because we live in the flesh and the spirit and the flesh are in opposition to each other. Jesus understood this. We read that He was tempted in all ways but didn't sin. He was fully God, fully man, and fully Holy Spirit. We are not, but are in the process of being transformed into His image. That transformation comes in the presence of the all-consuming fire of God.

Some of us have seen a couple in a marriage ceremony hold separate candles and light a third candle to burn as one flame representing their unity. The word of God uses the imagery of a bride and groom to symbolize the Lord's love for all believers—the church. Those who have been baptized by the holy fire of God in essence burn as one flame, and when we come to His consuming fire, we then burn as one with Him. In the high priestly prayer of John 17, Jesus prayed that we would be one as He was one with the Father. When we come into His presence with reverence and godly fear to serve Him, then we become one in the fire of His Holy Spirit. The nature of the triune God is such that Father, Son, and Holy Spirit are one in three. The privilege of all believers is to be able to enter in to this mystery. We can only have glimpses of that reality now. As a classic hymn says it is a "foretaste of love divine." We are not meant to experience this all the time, only as the Spirit wills. The times that I have had this profound experience have been the catalyst for working on this book. It is like an oasis to my thirsty soul in the desert of this life. Nothing can compare with the fullness of joy in the Lord's presence.

Unfortunately, many will not submit to this fire. Perhaps they have the wrong understanding of godly fear. Maybe they have never understood what it means to be in awe of God. I'm concerned that too much of what is happening in churches today has eliminated the reverential respect that the Lord is worthy of. Personally, I appreciate being casual in dress at church but not casual in attitude. I long for a solemn assembly where our hearts and minds and bodies can be stilled in His presence. I've known that stillness in my personal prayer time and a few times at church. I hope for the day when God's people are so consumed by Him individually that corporately we are consumed in worshipping Him. When Solomon's temple was dedicated, the people praised the Lord with one voice. His fire descended and the His glory was so powerful the priests could not stand up to minister.

Too often, what begins in the Spirit ends in the flesh. It's worse when despite good intentions, a move of God is perpetuated without the Spirit, usually for the sake of large congregations. So much of what is happening in churches is based on an agenda, system, or tradition. Praise God for the faithful who flock together to worship and learn. I am only praying to see the day when, if the Lord wants only worship, the program is dropped. If the Lord wants silence, all the sound equipment is unplugged. If the Lord wants dancing, we can do so without being inhibited or worldly. If the Lord just wants us to read His word, we would do it.

Consider the people weeping over hearing the word read for hours in the book of Ezra. I want to see the new thing God wants to do. I want to hear what the Spirit is saying to the churches today. I want to see the Lord move outside the four walls of a church building in new and creative ways that will impact our society and culture. I want to see God move in such a way that His people will never be the same. It will come with the willingness to let it all be burned away in the all-consuming passion of the fire of our God who is full of love, mercy, grace, and compassion.

19

JAMES

THE TONGUE IS A FIRE

My brethren, be not many masters, knowing that we shall receiver the greater condemnation. For in many things we offend all. If any man offend not in word, the same is a perfect man, *and* able to also bridle the whole body. Behold, we put bits in the horses' mouths, that they may obey us: and we turn their whole body. Behold the ships, which though *they be* so great, and *are* driven of fierce winds, yet are they turned about with a very small helm, whithersoever the governor listeth. Even so, the tongue is a little member, and boasteth great things. Behold, how great a matter a little fire kindleth! And the tongue *is* a fire, a world of iniquity: so is the tongue among our members, that it defileth the whole body, and setteth on fire the course of nature; and it is set on fire of hell. (James 3:1–6)

If ever life's circumstances and challenges collided with the study of these verses...now would be the time. My son, Tommy, has said, "Once taught, twice learned." Guess I really need to learn how to control my tongue. To be honest, I'm not doing a very good job. I've been challenged being the caregiver for my husband since his kidney transplant. To his credit, my husband just keeps pressing on, but he can be so intense and he makes me worry and I get upset.

At the same time, I'm going through menopause and I can be all over the place emotionally. How does this all fit in with James warning us about our tongues? Well, it's embarrassing to admit that my language would fall in the category of the expletives that need to be deleted. I already have some ideas for my next book called *Menopause: Puberty in Reverse*. The phrase "beside myself" has taken on a whole new meaning during this time. Sometimes, I feel like a teenager throwing a tantrum when I'm shouting, stomping my feet and slamming things around. Then I'm on my knees asking for forgiveness and help. It's all too real and I praise God for my girlfriends who are transparent enough to let me know I'm not alone. So there, I'm doing what the word says and that is to confess our sins to one another. No, I don't have it wired and even though I'd love to think I'm so spiritual...these last few years have really showed me how desperately I am in need of a savior and His Holy Spirit to change me. I want to be used by God so here I am again with a broken and contrite spirit.

The unusual circumstances that have merged with this study are that we just got some horses and are in the process of learning how to train them and be trained to ride them ourselves. I once heard meekness compared to a horse being ridden as controlled strength. Unfortunately, because we are new to this, my husband was bucked off and broke five ribs. So once again I am the caregiver to a man, who pushes the envelope to get "back in the saddle."

One of the dangers of broken ribs is that it can lead to pneumonia because breathing is shallow. Last night, he had intense pain with all the congestion. This morning, he wants to be outside while it's cold and raining. I want to scream at the top of my lungs, "Are you crazy?" He acts like he completely forgets that he is on drugs that suppress his immune system. I've lived with him for forty-two years and I wish the gentle approach worked. Usually, not until I get mad and then sad because I got mad does it really register with him.

There's a book called the *Five Love Languages*. Well, I think there should be another book called the *Five Anger Languages* because I'm trying to understand how to resolve conflicts. I remember all the yelling when I was a kid, but we always worked it out. John's family tended to do the silent treatment after the harsh treatment. I always thought there could be a happy medium to work through stuff. Now, I realize he just doesn't want to go there and that's who and how he is, and even though I need to deal with the issue, I need to figure out how not to lose it. I'm almost sixty and still trying to get it right. How can I be angry and not sin with my tongue? What's so bottled up inside me that I explode like a soda being shook spraying my husband with deplorable language? How's this for purging on paper?

Meanwhile, "back at the ranch," I'm thinking about that bit that goes on the horse's tongue and how I could use one these days. Maybe I need to imagine the Holy Spirit as the bit on my tongue because I certainly can't do it myself. It will be just like everything else He has helped me overcome. I remember seeing a rerun of a Pat Robertson show from the '70s. Corrie Ten Boom was his guest and as she was interviewed every word that came out of her mouth was scripture. That was more than ten years ago and I said to myself then that someday I want to speak like that.

So to finish this string of coincidences, guess what my personal Bible study is for today? Proverbs 15 starts off with: "A soft answer turneth away wrath: but grievous words stir up anger." Verse 4 reads, "A wholesome tongue *is* a tree of life: but perverseness therein is a breach in the spirit." That one cuts to the quick and describes how I feel I'm letting down the Lord. A breach means several things according to the Encarta World English Dictionary, but the one that applies is: to fail to obey, keep, or preserve something, for example, a law or trust. The breach in the spirit is my breaking the trust that the Lord has in me to obey His word so that what I say imparts grace to the hearer. The breach in the spirit is my failure to preserve the cleanliness of the temple of the Holy Spirit. The only thing that helps is when I read again the first part of this verse. It says whoever can control his tongue is a perfect man. I know of only one perfect man and that is Jesus! However, I am challenged by another verse that says that we should be perfect as our Father in heaven is perfect.

In verse 8, it says that no man can tame the tongue because it is unruly, evil and full of deadly poison. Verse 13 goes on to say that whoever is wise and has knowledge will show it with good conversation in works with meekness and wisdom. And that wisdom, according to verse 17, is pure peaceable, gentle, easily entreated, full of mercy and good fruits, without partiality, without hypocrisy. This chapter finishes with "the fruit of righteousness is sown in peace of them that make peace." These verses remind me of what Galatians 5 says about the fruits of the Holy Spirit. Those fruits are love, joy, peace, longsuffering, gentleness, goodness, faith, meekness, and temperance. Those tongues that are uncontrolled are tongues of fire from hell, but the controlled tongues of fire from the Holy Spirit speak truth, peace, and love in gentleness, kindness, and meekness.

I am ashamed that I have done the worst thing and that is to curse my husband with the same tongue that I praise God with. I determined to be transparent in this second book and so I have. I am grateful that the Lord knows my struggles and now you do, too. More than anything, I am blessed to have a husband that continually forgives me, a heavenly Father that sees Jesus in me, and the Holy Spirit that will help me clean up my verbal act. Now I know why James began the chapter with the warning not to be many masters. If you want to teach on something, be assured you will be tested in that area and will also be held to a higher standard.

FLESH EATEN BY FIRE

> Go to now, *ye* rich men, weep and howl for your miseries that shall come upon *you*. Your riches are corrupted, and your garments are motheaten. Your gold and silver is cankered; and the rust of them shall be a witness against you, and shall eat your flesh as it were fire. Ye have heaped treasure, together for the last days. (James 5:1–3)

What do we know about James that would give us an indication as to why he felt it necessary to write this warning? According to my *Bible Dictionary*, it is generally believed that James, the brother of Jesus, wrote this book around 45 AD before the destruction of Jerusalem. He was considered a leader of the first church in Jerusalem by references found in Acts 12:17, 15:13, and 21:18. This book was written in Greek so its purity is unchallenged, but its style resembles that of the Hebrew prophets and parallels the Lord's use of nature for imagery. He wrote to console, warn, reform, correct, and encourage the early believers through their afflictions, persecutions, and dispersion. His speech recorded in Acts 15 shows how he attempted to smooth the religious transition for Jews who had become Christians.

James addressed the rich in several verses. In chapter 1 verses 9–11, we read, "Let the brother of low degree rejoice in that he is exalted: But the rich, in that he is made low: because as the flower of the grass he shall pass away." The beginning of chapter 2 speaks against treating people differently in an assembly because of their apparel or stature. In verses 5–9, we learn of how the poor were treated by the rich. James wrote,

> Hearken my beloved brethren, Hath not God chosen the poor of this world rich in faith, and heirs of the kingdom

which he hath promised to them that love him? But ye have despised the poor. Do not rich men oppress you, and draw you before the judgment seats? Do not they blaspheme that worthy name by the which ye are called? If ye fulfil the royal law according to the scripture, Thou shalt love thy neighbour as thyself, ye do well: But if ye have respect to persons, ye commit sin, and are convinced of the law as transgressors.

Fast forward to our day when, in my opinion, there is sufficient wealth in our world to relinquish poverty, but we face the same challenges the readers of James's letter did. The disparity between rich and poor has created a widening gap. It seems to me that fewer and fewer hands are collectively holding the overall available monies. Small town businesses, what I call Mom and Pop operations, are disappearing from the American landscape. Major corporations have forced them out. What has happened to our nation that grew out of farming communities that had mutual concern for their neighboring townsfolk? The cancer of making wealth a lifelong pursuit has diseased our culture. Internationally, greed roars among the wealthy to keep the lion's share of the profits while third world countries are being exploited for labor and barely earn enough money for food. Truly, the Lord wants to bless us and provide for us but I'm sure He never intended the pursuit of wealth to be our main objective. He told us to first seek His kingdom and righteousness and we will have everything else we need.

The rest of chapter 5 explains that the workers are abused and the wealthy don't hear their cries but the Lord does. It says that those that live in pleasure on the earth have condemned and killed the just that don't resist. A promise of hope for the afflicted comes in verses 7 and 8:

Be patient therefore, brethren, unto the coming of the Lord. Behold, the husbandman waiteth for the precious fruit of the earth, and hath long patience for it, until he

receive the early and latter rain. Be ye also patient; stablish
your hearts: for the coming of the Lord draweth nigh.

Truly, the prophetic intent is apparent making this message
relevant to us.

The current economic situation has given rise to companies
that sell food insurance in the event of terrorist attack or
natural disaster. This is no different than stockpiling food for a
doomsday scenario. I've even heard of a frozen vault in the Arctic
that contains the seeds for practically every plant on earth. On
television and radio, we are bombarded with commercials to
invest in gold as currencies all over the world are being devalued.
All is under the sovereign hand of God as nations gradually step
closer toward a global economic system. The gold and silver will
rust and those that trusted in it will feel as though their flesh is
being consumed by fire.

As I continue my walk with Jesus, I have no fear of any
economic, social, or political collapse because I know that it will
lead the way for the millennial reign of Christ. However, there
was a time, before I was born again, during a bad drug trip I read
Revelations and thought I should be able to figure out a way to
provide for my family without taking the mark of the beast.

Almost forty years later and after being self-employed, I have
seen the Lord provide for all my family's needs time and time
again. I know that whatever happens in this world, if I am alive
to see the institution of the antichrist system, my heavenly Father
knows my needs before I have even spoken them and He will take
care of my family just as He takes care of the birds of the air and
the lilies of the field. How often have we failed to see the Lord
move on our behalf while we struggled under our own means
to meet our own needs? In the last days, despite tribulation or
persecution, we need to be able to walk that walk of faith that
James spoke of. We need to be patient and establish our hearts as
we wait for the coming of the Lord.

20

1 AND 2 PETER

TRIED BY FIRE

Blessed *be* the Lord Jesus Christ, which according to his abundant mercy hath begotten us again unto a lively hope by the resurrection of Jesus Christ from the dead, To an inheritance incorruptible, and undefiled, and that fadeth not away, reserved in heaven for you, Who are kept by the power of God through faith unto salvation ready to be revealed in the last time, Wherein ye greatly rejoice, though now for a season if need be, ye are in heaviness through manifold temptations: That the trial of your faith, being much more precious than of gold that perisheth, though it be tried with fire, might be found unto praise and honour and glory at the appearing of Jesus Christ: (1 Peter 1:3–7)

Tears came this morning as my husband and I listened to a classic praise song about how we need the Lord. All that John has gone through as his faith has been tried by the holy fire of God overwhelmed me. The New International Version replaces "ye are in heaviness through manifold temptations" with the phrase "though now for a little while you may have had to suffer grief in all kinds of trials."

I started studying the word fire before my husband had a brain stem stroke in 1998. He learned how to walk and talk again and has to daily deal with not being able to smile on the right side of his face and has to tape one eye shut because it won't close. He loves children and laments that his grandchildren have never seen his real smile. In public, children are usually afraid of him because of the lack of symmetry in his face. Some children and adults will ask what happened and John has learned to deal with it but it is still painful. It's not just the emotional pain he deals with but also the physical pain.

Often he says, "I am so tired of the pain." He has neuropathy, which causes the nerves in his extremities to burn all the time. He lost feeling on the left side of his body and from a nerve biopsy he has no feeling in his right foot. John had a quadruple bypass heart surgery in 1993 and has recovered from the kidney transplant surgery of 2009. He has continual pain from both knees that need to be replaced but surgery is risky because of his heart. He has healed somewhat from the five broken ribs. However, I have watched him walk daily along our driveway and pray for each member of our family at the trees he named after them. He continues to push himself to work and ride an exercise bike. He's basically on chemotherapy with all the anti-rejection medicines he takes. Nausea and dizziness are a way of life for him and if that wasn't enough his hair has started to thin. Despite all this, he is still handsome to me.

We've both gone through physical and emotional pain, and even though we wouldn't have chosen those types of trials, we have also come to realize it has allowed us to experience a level of intimacy with Christ that we would have never known otherwise. I've seen John reading his Bible in the middle of the night because he couldn't sleep. He might have his moments but mostly he remains positive, hopeful, and thankful. He should be a pile of ashes from this trial by fire but instead a beauty has risen up in him like Isaiah wrote about in Chapter 61.

Philippians 3:10 lets us know if we want to be fully acquainted with Jesus, we must be willing to share in His suffering in order to share in His glory. If there is a cross of pain that the good Lord has chosen for us, then we as "living sacrifices" must take it up daily. Jesus knew "the joy that was set before Him," and so He endured the cross on our behalf. Even though John would love to be healed, he also knows he wouldn't have the ministry that he has to hurting people that God, in His sovereignty, has ordained. If God knew us before we were born and He providentially allows us to suffer, He also knew that we would be "to His praise and glory." We have had many opportunities to minister to those dying in hospitals and the only way family members can let go is by not wanting their loved ones to suffer anymore. Philippians also talks about being conformed to the death of Jesus. His body died but was resurrected and so shall our bodies. This is our "lively" hope and that is why Peter could write that despite trials we can "greatly rejoice for a season."

THE HEAVENS ON FIRE

But the heavens and the earth, which are now, by the same word are kept in store, reserved unto fire against the day of judgment and perdition of ungodly men. But, beloved, be not ignorant of this one thing, that one day *is* with the Lord as a thousand years, and a thousand years as one day. The Lord is not slack concerning his promise, as some men count slackness; but is longsuffering to usward, not willing that any should perish, but that all should come to repentance. But the day of the Lord will come as a thief in the night; in the which the heavens shall pass away with a great noise, and the elements shall melt with fervent heat, the earth also and the works that are therein shall be burned up. Seeing that all these things shall be dissolved, what manner of persons ought ye to be in all holy conversation and godliness, Looking for and hasting unto the coming of the day of God, wherein the heavens being on fire shall be dissolved, and the elements shall melt with fervent heat? (Peter 3:7–12)

Often when I just type the scriptures, I become aware of the intricacies of the Bible. What does it mean that the heavens and earth are now kept in store by the same word? In the beginning of this chapter, Peter encourages the readers of this letter to "stir up your pure minds" by remembering and being "mindful of the words" that were spoken by the holy prophets, and of the "commandment of us the apostles of the Lord and Saviour." In verse 5, we read about those scoffers who deny the Lord's return and are willfully ignorant of the fact that by the word of God, the heavens "were of old" and the earth stood out of the water and was in the water. Peter is making the comparison that just as the earth overflowed with water likewise by the same word the earth is being "reserved unto fire against the day of judgment and perdition of ungodly men." We see the prophetic vision Peter received through his words.

The heavens and earth are "kept in store" for the day of judgment when suddenly a "great noise" will announce the departure of the heavens. In Revelation 6:14, the imagery is of the heavens being rolled up like a scroll at the opening of the sixth seal when the mountains and islands are moved out of place on the great day of the Lord's wrath. Isaiah 34:4 reads, "And all the host of heaven shall be dissolved, and the heavens shall be rolled together as a scroll: and all their host shall fall down, as the leaf falleth off from the vine and as a falling *fig* from the fig tree."

John the Revelator must have been familiar with this prophecy of Isaiah because he also wrote in chapter 6 verse 13, "And the stars of heaven fell unto the earth, even as a fig tree casteth her untimely figs, when she is shaken of a mighty wind." Matthew 24 also aligns the passing away of the heavens and earth with the parable of the fig tree, which refers to Israel becoming a nation in 1948. Verse 34 says the generation that was alive to witness this event will not die before all the prophecies are fulfilled. A generation could be 40, 80, or even 120 years, so we are living in that time frame.

Providing another visual, Hebrews 1:10–12 reads,

> And, Thou, Lord, in the beginning hast laid the foundation of the earth: and the heavens are the works of thine hands: They shall perish; but thou remainest: and they all shall wax old as doth a garment; And as a vesture shalt thou fold them up, and they shall be changed: but thou art the same, and thy years shall not fail.

In rabbinical fashion, the Lord answered Job in the form of questions found in chapter 38, which is a marvelous account of creation. In one question, God asked Job if he was there when He made the clouds a garment for the earth and "thick darkness a swaddlingband for it."

The imagery of the Hebrew language in the first chapter of Genesis revealed in essence that that garment marks the beginning of time, as we know it. When God spoke light into existence, He marked evening and morning as the first day by covering and uncovering the light. It wasn't until the fourth day He fashioned the sun and moon and stars and placed them in the firmament. On the second day, God made the firmament to divide the waters above from the waters below. The waters below were gathered together to let dry land appear which was called earth on the third day. I believe the waters below the firmament represent the clouds that wrap the earth like a garment. The word vesture is more like a cloak over the garment and would refer to what God used in creation to cover and uncover the light of the first day.

Paul wrote of a third heaven in Corinthians as where he was "caught up to paradise" in 2 Corinthians 12:2–3. So what is the first and second heaven? I see this in two ways. There is the atmospheric realm of the clouds under the firmament as the first. Then there is the realm in which Satan called in Ephesians 2:2 as "the prince of the power of the air," exercises his spiritual influence as the second. And the third is where the Lord sits on His throne. The other way to look at the three heavens would be to see the first one being as being that of creation before the fall; the second one as it is now; and the third heaven as that which is to come.

Peter repeats the phrase, "the elements shall melt with fervent heat." Once, he says that everything on the earth will be burned up and dissolved. Another time, he says the heavens will be on fire and dissolved. The elements are earth, air, water, and fire. We can imagine the earth being melted or burned with heat. This fervent heat could be the only real global warming that will occur so we could imagine the water that will melt as coming from the ice on the polar regions. We also know fire needs air to burn so we can imagine the air being on fire, but how can we imagine fire being on fire? The only biblical reference I can think of is in Ezekiel. We read in verse 4, "And I looked, and, behold, a whirlwind came out of the north, a great cloud, and a fire infolding itself, and a brightness *was* about it and out of the midst therof as the colour of amber, out of the midst of the fire."

The cloak of time will be folded up, the firmament will be dissolved and expose the eternal flame that will burn the elements in judgment so those who believe in the promises of God will see righteousness dwell in the new heaven and earth.

21

JUDE

PULLED OUT OF THE FIRE

Even as Sodom and Gomorrah, and the cites about them in like manner, giving themselves over to fornication, and going after strange flesh, are set forth for an example, suffering the vengeance of eternal fire…But ye, beloved, building up yourselves on your most holy faith, praying in the Holy Ghost, Keep yourselves in the love of God, looking for the mercy of our Lord Jesus Christ unto eternal life. And of some have compassion, making a difference: And others save with fear, pulling them out of the fire; hating even the garment spotted by the flesh. (Jude 1:7, 20–23)

There are cities in this world that I would compare to Sodom and Gomorrah and it was in one of them that I learned the most powerful spiritual lesson. It was during what I now call my "holier than thou" stage. I was totally entrenched in a Christian subculture. I had a Christian husband, my children were

Christian, and I worked at a Christian radio station and went to church three sometimes four days a week. All my friends were Christians. I would burn my candles and frankincense, play my Christian music, and wouldn't pray unless I had bathed first. It was pharisaical and I was a "stench in God's nostrils" thinking that all my machinations made me holy.

At the time, my daughter was a fitness competitor and she invited us to a competition in Las Vegas, Nevada. I thought, *I could never go to such a sinful place.* Since I wanted to support my daughter, we ended up going with our family. It was definitely a challenge to be there. One evening, my husband and I wanted to find a place to eat. We heard someone singing some familiar songs from the sixties. Of course, I was "convicted" of listening to secular music because I programmed Christian music. It was in the fall so the evening was cold, but this outdoor restaurant/bar had some fire pits around the dance floor. There were lots of young people dancing as the singer did his best renditions of the classic hits.

In the middle of the dance floor was a woman considerably older than the rest who was dancing with no one and everyone at the same time. She was seriously drunk and dancing lewdly while everyone was laughing at her. Eventually, she was the only one dancing. I was watching this unfold behind the comfort of my fire pit when an image was burned in my mind forever. I saw her burning in the fires of hell and my heart was broken. When I shared with her that Jesus loved her, she said, "Oh yeah, I love Jesus." I gave her a bracelet that had a cross on it and told her to remember how much He loved her. When we got to the parking garage, I had the most intense grief wash over me that I can only explain as a glimpse of the sorrow God the Father has for all his children who are lost.

I left Las Vegas ashamed of my self-righteousness and vowed to always remember that night and that woman. I know I cannot save anyone but to think that according to this passage we as believers can pull someone out of the fire is amazing. John and I have our own personal mission. We want to love the lost and serve the saints. We walk in two worlds even though we are not of this world we are in this world, and I pray always that God's people will learn how to reach the lost. It scares me to this day to think of how lost I was, all the while thinking I was okay.

If the enemy tries to drag me down by reminding me of my sinful past, I have learned to use that to keep me humble and to rest in the work of the cross. I remember searching every New Age avenue and only finding dead ends. My heart breaks for those under such delusions. I remember the numbing pang of alcohol and the euphoric confusion of drugs. On two occasions, I know that Satan as an "angel of light" came to bargain with me. I praise the Lord for all He allowed to break the chains of bondage to my will and flesh.

The lust of the flesh is what this book deals with, those who serve themselves. Our society is consumed with the lust of the flesh, the lust of the eyes, and the pride of life. But here we learn that we must build up our most holy faith by praying in the Holy Ghost, by keeping in God's love, and by waiting for the Lord's mercy and eternal life. The Bible tells us that if we sow to the flesh we will bring corruption, but if we sow to the spirit we will bring life. The flesh is degenerating. We have a choice daily, even moment by moment to give in to the flesh or not by resisting temptation, holding our thoughts captive and by building up our faith.

It requires discipline to turn away from many of the things we see daily that can tempt us. As a reminder to myself, I have categorized the three main temptations as food, fame (fortune comes with that), and fate. This is how Jesus was tempted and we are told that He was tempted in all ways but never sinned. We don't have to hide in shame for being tempted but the enemy would like us to. We are promised a way out of that temptation in the simple principle of resisting the devil, and he will leave us alone and as we draw closer to God He draws closer to us. Don't ever think because you blow it you can't run to Jesus. He understands everything we are going through. I believe that's why He chose to clothe His divinity with flesh and bones. The discipline of resisting becomes second nature when the Holy Spirit leads us. It is His control that gives us self-control. Rather let us be overcome by God's love and mercy as we wait for the deliverance of eternal life in the presence of the Triune God.

22

REVELATION

EYES AS A FLAME OF FIRE

And I turned to see the voice that spake with me. And being turned, I saw seven golden candlesticks; And in the midst of the seven candlesticks *one* like unto the Son of man, clothed with a garment down to the foot, and girt about the paps with a golden girdle. His head and *his* hairs *were* white like wool, as white as snow; and his eyes *were* as a flame of fire; And his feet like unto fine brass, as if they burned in a furnace; and his voice as the sound of many waters. And he had in his right hand seven stars: and out of his mouth went a sharp twoedged sword: and his countenance was as the sun shineth in his strength. (Revelation 1:12–16)

And unto the angel of the church in Thyatira write; These things saith the Son of God, who hath his eyes like unto a flame of fire and his feet *are* like fine brass: I know thy works, and charity, and service, and faith, and thy patience, and thy works; and the last *to be* more than the first. (Revelation 2:18)

And I saw heaven opened, and behold a white horse; and he that sat upon him *was* called Faithful and True, and in righteousness he doth judge and make war. His eyes were as a flame of fire, and on his head *were* many crowns; and he had a name written, that no man knew, but he himself. And he *was* clothed with a vesture dipped in blood: and his name is called The Word of God…And out of his mouth goeth a sharp sword, that with it he should smite the nations: and he shall rule them with a rod of iron: and he treadeth the winepress of the fierceness and wrath of Almighty God. And he hath on *his* vesture and on his thigh a name written, King of kings, and Lord of lords. (Revelation 19:11–13, 15–16)

John began this book with the phrase "the Revelation of Jesus Christ." The Greek word used for revelation is where the word apocalypse comes from and it is derived from a root word that means to take off the cover, to disclose or reveal according to *Strong's Greek Dictionary of the New Testament.* Just as studying the Old Testament in the Hebrew yielded a bounty of information, likewise the Greek language provides a unique perspective. Previously, I wrote the Hebrew understanding of the first day of creation amounted to God's hand covering and uncovering the light spoken of into existence on the first day. The word for light could have been translated as fire.

In researching the word *Christ,* I learned it means the "anointed" and had its basis in words that mean: to consecrate; furnish what is needed; entreat; the hollowness of the hand and impassable interval. (Reference these Greek Lexicon Numbers as they trace the root meaning: 5547>5548>5530>5425>5495>5490) The Hebrew word for covering comes from a root word that means hallow or palm of the hand. I concluded the hand of God anoints us with the oil of His love to cover us and to bridge the otherwise impassable interval that leads to eternal life. At the beginning of the High Priestly Prayer found in John 17, Jesus said eternal life was to know the only true God and Jesus Christ whom He sent.

John begins writing with urgency for the "things which must shortly come to pass" to "bare record of the word of God, and of the testimony of Jesus Christ and of all things that he saw." This book comes with a promise of blessings to those who read, hear and keep the words of the prophecy. His introduction is a prayer as he speaks grace and peace to the seven churches in Asia from the One who is, was, and is to come; from the seven Spirits that are before His throne and from Jesus Christ. For a book that is full of judgment and wrath, it strikes me that John begins this way.

Revelation 4:5 explains the seven Spirits of God are seven lamps of fire burning before the throne in heaven. Jesus is described as the faithful witness, the first begotten of the dead, the prince of the kings of the earth. He was the one who loved us and washed us from our sins in His own blood, and we have been made kings and priest to God and His Father. He is deserving of glory and dominion forever and ever. Then John writes of His return in 1:7–8,

> Behold, he cometh with clouds; and every eye shall see him and they *also* which pierced him: and all kindreds of the earth shall wail because of him. Even so, Amen. (Then Jesus speaks:) I am Alpha and Omega, the beginning and the ending, saith the Lord, which is and which was, and which is to come, the Almighty.

The apostle saw these visions while in exile on the Isle of Patmos. John, as a "brother and companion in tribulation and patience of Jesus Christ," was "in the Spirit on the Lord's day" when he heard a great voice that sounded like a trumpet behind him. I'm sure John meant something more similar to a ram's horn that was blown at Jewish celebrations. Likewise, in Matthew 24 when the Lord is seen in the clouds and all the tribes on earth mourn, He will send His angels to gather the elect with the sound of a great trumpet. I also have to wonder if he meant a day of rest set aside to worship the Lord or the day of the Lord. When he turned, he saw one like the Son of man standing in the middle of seven golden candlesticks. The candlesticks are the seven churches that John is instructed to write to about the things he saw—the things that are and the things that would occur hereafter.

John's description of Jesus is somewhat similar to what Daniel said of the Ancient of Days found in chapter 7 verse 9. His garment was white as snow and His hair was like pure wool and He sat on a fiery throne. The verses we are addressing in this section tell of three instances in Revelation where John mentions the Lord's eyes looked like flames of fire. Also in chapter 10 verse 5, Daniel also spoke of seeing a "certain man" wearing linen and gold with a body of beryl, a face like lightning and eyes like "lamps of fire" with arms and feet like polished brass and a voice that sounded like a multitude. (See Fire in the Bible: Genesis to Daniel for a detailed study on these verses.)

While seven is the most prominent number repeated in Revelation, I believe it's relevant; we are told of the eyes of fire three times. Perhaps the events surrounding those occurrences might give insight. The first time John sees Jesus, it's in the middle of the seven candlesticks relating to the seven churches. The second time is when Jesus speaks to the church of Thyatira. This church specifically was chastised for indulging the Jezebel of end times that calls herself a prophetess and seduces the Lord's servant to commit fornication and to eat things sacrificed to idols. The third time is when the Lord comes with the armies of heaven to the throw the beast and false prophet and those who fought for them into the lake of fire. All three events involve fire!

John fell down as if he were dead when he saw the Lord but was told not to fear because He is the first and last. He continues in verse 18, "I *am* he that liveth, and was dead; and, behold, I am alive for evermore, Amen; and have the keys of hell and of death." Before we hear of all the judgments and wrath, we are told not to fear. Many struggle with understanding the visions of the Lord and whether to take them literally or not. I believe it was as it was written. I often wonder why the Lord would open my eyes spiritually to see Him and to see the visions of fire that He has shown me. It is a blessing to have been given this insight. I have always tried to line up what I have seen and heard with the Word of God and not to trust my own understanding. I believe God is the rewarder of those that diligently seek Him. There is so much controversy and confusion surrounding the book of Revelation, and by the grace of God, I hope and pray to dispel it as we continue searching the remaining fire verses and attempt to put the pieces together of this amazing prophetic puzzle.

GOLD TRIED IN THE FIRE

I counsel thee to buy of me gold tried in the fire, that thou mayest be rich; and white raiment, that thou mayest be clothed, and *that* the shame of thy nakedness do not appear; and anoint thine eyes with eyesalve, that thou mayest see. (Revelation 3:18)

This verse is from the seventh letter to the seventh church mentioned in chapters 2 and 3 of the Revelation of Jesus Christ. Each church was rebuked except the church of Philadelphia. Each church was given promises if they would endure and overcome. Once, it struck me that the promises that are given to the seven churches are promises we as believers already have. As a result, I did a study called Seven Letters-Seven Years, which follows. It occurred to me that each church could correspond to each year of the tribulation. I'm aware of commentaries that speak of each of these churches representing the different church ages. But once again, I say the promises given are promises we have already received when we accepted Jesus as Lord and Savior.

Ephesus is promised the tree of life; Smyrna is promised the crown of life and not to be hurt by the second death; Pergamos is promised to eat of the hidden manna and to be given a white stone with a new name that no one knows; Thyatira is promised power over the nations to rule with a rod of iron breaking the nations in pieces; Sardis is promised to be clothed in white and that their names will not be blotted out of the book of life and that the Lord will confess them before His father; Philadelphia is promised to be pillars in the temple of God; Laodicea is promised to sit at the throne even as Jesus overcame and has sat down with His father in His throne.

Originally, the seven churches were closely connected politically, commercially, religiously, and geographically. Their history also reveals similarities to events that will occur during the end times. Ephesus was a city in Lydia that worshipped Artemis, a nature goddess, built a temple to Diana and had a permissive society. In Smyrna, Bishop Polycarp suffered martyrdom by fire in 169 AD and an earthquake destroyed the city, a commercial center, in 178 AD. The statue of Zeus and the temple of Athens were in Pergamum as well as a shrine of healing were people flocked. It was considered a stronghold of Christian idolatry. Sardis was colonized with Greeks and was known for the skill of dyeing fabrics purple. It was a sandstone citadel burned by the Athenians, invaded by Persians, and ruled by the Greeks and Romans and ruined by earthquakes. Philadelphia was destroyed by an earthquake in 17 AD but rebuilt. Laodicea was once considered the city of Zeus. A medical school there had physicians who prepared Phrygian powder to cure eye diseases. It was also destroyed by an earthquake but rebuilt without the help of the Romans.

Likewise, each church has characteristics that correspond with the progression of prophetic events during the tribulation. The Ephesian church is told to return to their "first love" representing the first year of the tribulation. The pagan influences did and will turn their hearts away from Jesus. Consider Matthew 24:12 that warns in the last days the love of many will grow cold because sin is so rampant. Smyrna, representing the second year of the tribulation, is exhorted to remain constant in the midst of persecution. Jesus warned them to endure till the end. The word Pergamos means bigamy representing a church funded by the government where Satan's throne is as the third year of the tribulation when the abomination of desolation is set up as spoken of in Matthew 24:15. The following verses speak of the days being shortened for the elect's sake, the powers of heaven and earth being shaken and the appearing of the Son of man. The church of Thyatira, indicative of the fourth year of the tribulation, suffers the Jezebel influence representing the mystery religion of Babylon. However, not all in this church ascribe to this satanic doctrine and are told to hold fast to the true doctrine. The tribulation's fifth year church is Sardis, and it is told they live but are dead but have a few who have not been defiled and will walk with God in glory. They are told to be watchful and repent. The sixth year of the tribulation has the church of Philadelphia which will be kept from "the hour of temptation that comes upon the world." The seventh year of the tribulation has the lukewarm, poor, and naked church of Laodicea that considers itself to be rich and in need of nothing.

Jesus reveals Himself to the first church as having the seven stars in His right hand and is in the midst of the seven golden candlesticks. To Smyrna, He says, He is the first and the last and that He was dead but alive. He is the One with the sharp two-edged sword to Pergamos. To Thyatira, He is the Son of God who has eyes like a flame of fire. He is holy and true and has the key of David to open and shut what no one else can to Philadelphia.

He is Amen, faithful and true and the beginning of creation to Laodicea.

The first year of the tribulation, I align with Matthew 23:38 when Jesus says the temple is left desolate. The second year coincides with Matthew 24:1 as Jesus leaves the temple. The third year is when believers are persecuted for His name's sake in Matthew 24:9. The fourth year corresponds with Matthew 24:29 when the powers of heaven are shook. The fifth year compares with Matthew 24:43 when Jesus says He will come as a thief. The sixth year goes with Matthew 24:45 when the Lord makes the servant ruler. The seventh year is likened to Matthew 25:5 because they slept when the bridegroom came.

The complacency of the Laodicean church is the spiritual disease that blinded them to their spiritual poverty, blindness, and nakedness. The gold they needed had to be tried by fire. The Philadelphian church kept the word of God and did not deny the name of Jesus. The church of Sardis was told their works were not perfect and they needed to watch and be strong. Those of Thyatira, who did not follow Jezebel, were told to keep the Lord's works to the end. Pergamos was told to repent for its impure worship of idols. Sardis was warned not to fear the things they would suffer by imprisonment or tribulation. Ephesus was told to remember from where they had fallen, repent and to do the works they did at first.

Individually, we all can have the characteristics of these churches. I remember of one time in my life when I loved what I was doing for the Lord more than I loved Him. I firmly believe that there will be a church that will suffer persecution before the Lord returns. No revival will occur without persecution. Once the Lord spoke to me that there will be a time of favor before the persecution, a time of persecution before the revival, a time of revival before the tribulation, and a time of tribulation before the rapture.

I know that Satan will do anything to pervert the worship of the Holy One of Israel. All that this world has to offer is meant to distract us from praising God. Sometimes, our hearts have the wrong motives when we are working for the Lord. Tragically, being neither cold nor hot for the things of God will blind us to our pathetic condition. These letters have spoken through the ages and will speak to those who are alive to see the events of prophecy become fulfilled. As the Lord said, "He who has an ear let him hear what the spirit is saying to the churches."

SEVEN LAMPS OF FIRE

> And out of the throne proceeded lightnings and thunderings and voices: and *there were* seven lamps of fire burning before the throne, which are the seven Spirits of God. (Revelation 4:5)

Revelation 4 records the vision John saw as the door of heaven was opened. He is spoken to by the trumpet voice also heard in chapter 1 and told he would be shown the things that "must be hereafter." He describes the throne and the One who sat on it and mentions the twenty-four seats where the twenty-four elders sat in white clothing with crowns of gold. I believe this is a reference to the twelve patriarchs and the twelve apostles (including Paul) who lay their crowns before the throne and worship the Lord. In this chapter, we also read of the four beasts who are full of eyes before and behind that never rest saying, "Holy, holy, holy Lord God Almighty, which was, and is and is to come."

There are a few other scriptures that refer to the seven spirits of God. Revelation 1:4, "John to the seven churches which are in Asia: Grace *be* unto you, and peace, from him which is, and which was, and which is to come; and from the seven Spirits which are before the throne." Revelation 3:1, "And unto the angel of the church in Sardis write; These things saith he that hath the seven

Spirits of God, and the seven stars; I know thy works, that thou hast a name that thou livest, and art dead." Revelation 5:6, "And I beheld, and, lo, in the midst of the throne and of the four beast, and in the midst of the elders, stood a Lamb as it had been slain, having seven horns and seven eyes, which are the seven Spirits of God sent forth into all the earth."

In Zechariah, the seven eyes and seven lamps are written of in chapters 3 and 4. The context of these verses is within the vision that is given concerning the reconstruction of the temple. Joshua was the high priest and Zerubbabel was the governor in Judah who were commanded by the word of the Lord through Haggai to rebuild the temple because of the destruction of Solomon's temple by the Babylonians. Initially, we are told Zechariah sees Satan who was there to resist Joshua but the Lord rebukes him. Joshua is given clean clothes and is told by the Lord of host to walk in His ways and keep His charge so he will able to judge the Lord's house.

Apparently, there are others standing by in this vision because we learn that these men are "wondered at" and Joshua will walk among them. The promise is given for the Branch, a reference to Jesus. Zechariah 3:9 reads, "For behold the stone that I have laid before Joshua; upon one stone *shall be* seven eyes; behold, I will engrave the graving thereof, saith the Lord of hosts, and I will remove the iniquity of that land in one day." Zechariah is asked to describe what he sees by an angel. He sees a golden candlestick that has seven lamps on it that are being fed by pipes from seven bowls which get their oil from two olive trees on either side.

When Zechariah asks for an explanation, he is told: "This is the word of the Lord unto Zerubbabel, saying, Not by might, nor by power, but by my spirit, saith the Lord of hosts." In what appears to be an analogy of the opposition they will face in rebuilding the temple, we are told that the Lord will make the mountain a plain, and as the headstone is brought forth, there will be shouts of "Grace, grace" for it. Zerubbabel was to lay the foundation of the house and finish it. The work began in 537 BC but was interrupted in 534, resumed in 520 only to be completed in 515. Zechariah would know that the Lord of hosts had been sent to him. Verse 10 reads, "For who hath despised the day of small things? for they shall rejoice, and shall see the plummet in the hand of Zerubbabel *with* those seven; they *are* the eyes of the Lord, which run to and fro through the whole earth. When Zechariah questions the angel about the two olive trees, he is told they are the two anointed ones that stand by the Lord of the whole earth. Revelation 11 tells of the two anointed ones who will prophesy for three and a half years during the tribulation. Although some teach these two are Moses and Elijah, I point to this vision as evidence of two others. Sometimes, I've wondered if they could be Jesus and the Holy Spirit. Zechariah saw the same vision that John saw of what appears to be a menorah, a Jewish candlestick. The flames of these candles or lamps are compared to the seven eyes of the Lord just as we read that the Lord's eyes looked like flames of fire.

Once again, I put forth the concept in eschatology called "near and far fulfillment." Haggai, the prophet to Joshua and Zerubbabel, spoke of the rebuilding of the temple and I use chapter 2 verses 6–9 to speak of the new temple that will be built for the millennial reign. It reads,

> For thus saith the Lord of hosts: Yet once, it *is* a little while, and I will shake, the heavens, and the earth, and the sea, and the dry *land*; and I will shake all nations, and the desire of all nations shall come: and I will fill this house with glory, saith the Lord of hosts. The silver *is* mine, and the gold *is* mine, saith the Lord of hosts. The glory of this latter house shall be greater than of the former, saith the Lord of hosts: and in this place will I give peace, saith the Lord of hosts.

Hebrews 12:25–29 reads,

See that ye refuse not him that speaketh. For if they escaped not who refused him that spake on earth, much more *shall not* we turn away from him that *speaketh* from heaven: Whose voice then shook the earth: but now he hath promised, saying, Yet once more I shake not the earth only, but also heaven. And this *word,* Yet once more, signifieth the removing of those things that are shaken, as of things that are made, that those things which cannot be shaken may remain. Wherefore we receiving a kingdom which cannot be moved, let us have grace, whereby we may serve God acceptably with reverence and godly fear: For our God *is* a consuming fire.

Isaiah 11:1–2 reads,

And there shall come forth a rod out of the stem of Jesse, and a Branch shall grow out of his roots: And the spirit of the Lord shall rest upon him, the spirit of wisdom and understanding, the spirit of counsel and might, the spirit of knowledge and of the fear of the Lord.

This chapter speaks of the second time the Lord will come to gather the remnant of His people. Verse 12 says, "And he shall set up an ensign for the nations, and shall assemble the outcasts of Israel, and gather together the dispersed of Judah from the four corners of the earth." Chapter 12 verse 6 confirms the presence of the Lord when it says, "Cry out and shout, thou inhabitant of Zion; for great *is* the Holy One of Israel in the midst of thee." Just as when Zechariah saw the man with a measuring line in his hand measuring the breadth and length of Jerusalem and was told: "Jerusalem shall be inhabited *as* towns without walls for the multitude of men and cattle therein: For I saith the Lord, will be unto her a wall of fire round about, and will be the glory in the midst of her." Just as John was told in Revelation 11 to measure the temple of God during the time when the two anointed ones will prophesy, those who are alive to see these things transpire must be able to endure the tribulation to be able to inhabit Jerusalem during the thousand years of peace when Jesus will reign.

Once at a Newsboys concert in the mid-nineties as I watched a crowd of young people celebrate the Lord's presence in their midst, I heard the Lord say, "This is the generation that will usher in the millennium." The time is drawing near. The prelude events are occurring at an exponential rate. We are told to watch but to look up for our redemption is drawing closer every day.

FIRE OF THE ALTAR

> And the angel took the censer, and filled it with fire of the altar, and cast *it* into the earth: and there were voices, and thunderings, and lightnings, and an earthquake. (Revelation 8:5)

In chapter 5, John only sees the four living creatures, angels, and elders before the throne. In Revelation 6, the first four seals release the horsemen. The fifth seal reveals those slain under the altar that ask how long until their fellow servants are killed as they were. The opening of the sixth seal brings the great earthquake when the sun becomes black, the moon becomes as blood, and the stars fall. It is also when the heavens depart and are rolled up like a scroll, the mountains and the islands are moved out of their place, and men hide in caves wishing the mountains would fall on them. This is the great day of wrath of the Lamb. After this, the tribes of Israel are sealed so no harm will come to them. I believe this is when the church is raptured.

In Chapter 7, John sees the great multitude before the throne, and in verse 14, it says they have come out of the great tribulation and their robes were washed and made white by the blood of the Lamb. This multitude, made up of all nations, kindreds, peoples, and tongues is before the throne of God. The Lamb in their midst will feed them and lead them to the living fountains of water and God will wipe every tear from their eyes. As well as in Revelation 21:4, we read that God will wipe away every tear from those who inhabit the New Jerusalem.

So when the seventh seal is opened, there is silence for half an hour. Before the seven trumpets sound, the angel with the censer comes. The censer is first filled with incense, this being the prayers of the saints, and is offered on the golden altar before the throne. I can't help but wonder about the prayers that were offered up before the next event happened. Then smoke went up before God out of the angel's hand, and then he filled it with fire from the altar and threw it on the earth causing the voices, thunderings, lightnings, and earthquakes.

There are several other times in Revelation when we read of the voices, thunderings, lightnings, and earthquakes. In chapter 4 verse 5, John describes the scene in heaven when the door was opened and he was "in the spirit" as he saw the rainbow encircling the throne and the one who sat on it all appearing as an emerald. He also saw the elders clothed in white wearing gold crowns. Out of the throne "proceeded lightnings and thunderings and voices." There is no mention of earthquakes in this vision. In chapter 11 verse 19, we read, "And the temple of God, was opened in heaven, and there was seen in his temple the ark of his testament: and there were lightnings, and voices and thunderings, and an earthquake and great hail." This scene follows the death of the two witnesses who were killed by the beast that came out of the bottomless pit. After three and a half days until the "Spirit of life from God" brought them back to life and they ascended causing all who rejoiced over their death to be filled with great fear. We are told the great earthquake that followed with seven thousand being slain and the rest giving God glory is the second woe. The third woe follows the declaration of the great voices of heaven after the seventh trumpet is blown. All dominion is given to Christ and all the elders fall on their faces to worship the Lord

God Almighty who was and is and is to come for having taken His power and reigned. Verse 18 reads,

> And the nations were angry, and thy wrath is come, and the time of the dead, that they should be judged, and that thou shouldest give reward unto thy servants the prophets and to the saints, and them that fear thy name, small and great and shouldest destroy them which destroy the earth.

The mention of the bottomless pit and the time of judgment and reward in this vision confirm my understanding of the simultaneous unfolding of the prophetic events in Revelation. What John sees "in the spirit" is outside of our understanding of time. In the Old English translation of the Bible, the word "and" is used repeatedly. In newer translations, the word "then" is used instead. This change creates a sense of chronological order. As we read Revelation, it's almost as if we are watching seven different screens with seven seals being opened, seven trumpets being blown and seven bowls of wrath being poured out.

Let's line up these to see what happens: The first seal opened releases the man on a white horse who conquers with only a bow; the first trumpet blown causes a third part of the trees to be burned up by the hail and fire mingled with blood and the first bowl poured out causes those who have the mark of the beast to have terrible sores. The second seal releases the red horse and the rider is given a great sword to take peace from the earth so that people will kill each other; the second trumpet makes a third part of the sea become blood killing a third of the life and ships when a fiery mountain is thrown into it and the second bowl was poured on the sea and it became like blood so every living soul in it died. The third seal releases the black horse with scales who controls the price of wheat and barley and cautions not to hurt the oil and wine; the third trumpet announces the falling of the star called Wormwood that kills a third part of the men because it makes a third of the rivers and fountains of waters bitter and the third bowl makes the rivers and fountains of water like blood. The fourth seal reveals a pale horse with a rider name Death with Hell following over a fourth part of the earth to kill with sword, hunger, death and the beast of the earth; the fourth trumpet causes a third part of the day and night to be covered in darkness because a third of the sun, moon and stars was darkened and the fourth bowl was poured out on the sun and the fourth angel that did this was able to scorch men with fire. The fifth seal reveals the souls of the martyrs waiting to be avenged under the altar being told to rest until their fellowservants and brethren would be killed as they were; the fifth trumpet causes a "star" to fall who releases and army of locusts ruled by a king named, Abbadon or in Greek, Apollyon, and the fifth bowl was poured out on the "seat of the beast" creating darkness and gnawing pain in his kingdom. The sixth seal tells of the day of wrath of the Lamb when there is a great earthquake and the sun is blackened, the moon turns the color of blood, the stars fall and the heavens depart, and the mountains and islands are moved, and the sixth trumpet loses the four angels bound by the river Euphrates to kill a third part of men by the fire, smoke, and brimstone that comes out of their mouth as they ride on horses with lion heads and the sixth bowl was poured out on the river Euphrates to dry it up so the "way of the kings of the east might be prepared." The seventh seal brings a half hour of silence in heaven; the seventh trumpet announces that "the mystery of God should be finished, as he hath declared to his servants the prophets," and before the seventh bowl is poured out, John is told not to write what the seven thunders say then the angel pours his bowl into the air and "there came a great voice out of the temple of heaven, from the throne, saying, It is done." Then once again in chapter 16 verses 18–19, we read,

> And there were voices, and thunders, and lightnings; and
> there was a great earthquake, such as not since men were

upon the earth, so mighty an earthquake, *and* so great. And the great city was divided into three parts, and the cities of the nations fell: and great Babylon came in remembrance before God, to give unto her the cup of the wine of the fierceness of his wrath.

While many try to line up everything in some sort of sequential order, we see how some of the events are related, even similar. It is so intriguing to consider this book. I am continually fascinated by it and try to put myself in John's place as he viewed what we are seeing transpire today. It's amazing that God would allow him a glimpse into the future—a future that has its present in eternity past. When the seven thunders utter their voices, we learn that "time would be no longer." Time is linear and basically intersects with eternity. In Genesis 1, we read of how God created the sun, moon, and stars for signs and seasons and days and years. When these lesser and greater lights no longer exist, neither will time as we know it.

Try to imagine all this activity in John's visions happening before the throne in heaven and before the ark of His testament in the temple. In Revelation 13:8, we are told "the Lamb was slain before the foundation of the earth." The fire and the altar that are used to bring offerings to God are also used to bring destruction to the earth and to those whose names are not written in the Lamb's Book of Life.

HAIL AND FIRE MINGLED WITH BLOOD

The first angel sounded, and there followed hail and fire mingled with blood, and they were cast upon the earth: and the third part of trees was burnt up, and all green grass was burnt up. (Rev. 8:7)

This first angel is one of seven John sees receiving trumpets before God during the half hour of silence after the seventh seal is opened. The seventh seal and first trumpet seem to segue in chapter 8. Consider it an overlapping transition. This hail, fire, and blood follow the fire of the altar thrown on earth producing voices, thunderings, lightnings, and earthquakes written of in the previous section. The results of the first trumpet precede the great mountain of fire that causes the sea to become blood.

The thought of hail and fire mingled with blood is very disgusting to imagine. It would be like burning blood raining upon the earth. Why would only a third of the trees be burned up? Why is all the green grass burned? I often think this is a purging of the earth before the millennial earthly reign of Christ. Controversy abounds as to whether the earth, as we know it, is a "world without end" or whether as Peter said all the elements will be burned up. The elements are earth, air, water, and fire. Revelation tells us in the end there will be a new heaven and a new earth without a sea. Our imaginations are taken to task as we try to visually understand what the visions of Revelation are describing.

I am reminded of the prophetic warning in 2 Kings 21:13 because of the abominations done in Solomon's temple and for the blood on the streets at the hand of Manasseh who ruled fifty-five years in Jerusalem after Hezekiah, Jerusalem would be cleansed by God's hand as if He were wiping a dish. The news for the day as I began working on this section tells of Middle East outrage over the Israelis claiming two historic sites by the Dome of the Rock. Tragically, there is no support from the United States under the Obama administration instead there is condemnation. When Zechariah prophesied all nations would come against Israel that would include America, if it still exists, as we know it, when the prophetic events unfold. In little over a year, we have witnessed government intervention into almost every sector of private life. The campaign promise of change is being delivered at an alarming rate with sweeping reforms being made in industry, healthcare, finance, immigration, and energy all at the expense of the citizen's through incredible taxation.

As much as I want to believe in this nation as it was founded, I process all I hear and see through the grid of the word of God. If there is to be four ruling powers that become ten, that eventually give their power to the one, establishing a one world government, which imposes a one world religious system operating with a one world economic system, then our republic as we know it is in the beginning stages of its demise. As much as the states along the borders wish to maintain security, I see the dissolution of the borders as the next major prophetic event to transpire. The manufacturers of household products are already printing all their labels in French, English, and Spanish. The Canadian, American, and Mexican leaders already met during the Bush administration and again under Obama calling it the Three Amigos Summit. Although some try to discredit this move toward a North American Union along the lines of the European Union, I believe we are on the verge of seeing this become a reality. The constitution will be abolished and our currency will be converted to what has been called an Amero. The existing financial crisis has been constructed to bring about the destruction of our current economic system.

Anyone that listens to liberal and conservative views in the media would see the attempt to divide this nation down political lines. A grassroots movement has risen up to oppose the agenda of this presidency but is being disparaged by the liberal media as racist. The conservative media sees the direction of the administration as socialist. I see this as an if/then moment in the life of this nation and in the life of the body of Christ in America.

At the dedication of Solomon's temple, the Lord made promises and warnings to His chosen people. Second Chronicles 7 tells the story of how God's presence was so powerful that when His fire came to burn up the sacrifice, neither the people nor the priest could stand up. After Solomon's prayer, the Lord appeared to him at night saying in verse 14, "If my people, which are called by my name, shall humble themselves, and pray, and seek my face, and turn from their wicked ways then will I hear from heaven, and will forgive their sin, and will heal their land." Notice the if/then in that passage. God's love is unconditional but his promises are conditional because He only wants the best for us. The history of the Jewish people shows how their rebellion and idolatry brought God's judgment. Sometimes it came by the hand of their enemies. I fear this is what will happen to America.

The blood on the streets of America is from the millions of babies that have been aborted just as the idolatry of Manasseh led to the sacrifice of children in the fires for worship to pagan gods. The sexual revolution brought about the sacrifice of infants to the gods of pleasure. Judgment is coming and it will bring about the end of the United States as we know it because prophecy will be fulfilled and nations will rise against nations and there will be wars and rumors of wars until the son of perdition rises up to bring about a false peace that seduces the nations into a holy covenant. The famines and pestilence will increase in ways that we cannot imagine. It occurred to me that cancer is a plague unlike any other just as the AIDS epidemic. The rain falls on the just and the unjust and God is sovereign through it all. So often I hear of ministries promising a way out of a financial or medical crisis and it could very well be the means by which God draws one closer to Him.

Just as in the days of Noah, people will go on living their lives until the floods come. The next time, it will be a flood of blood mingled with fire. Those who loved the lie of the enemy and were deluded because of the hardness of their hearts will be left outside the ark of the covenant of rescue. The Lord told us there would be tribulation but He had overcome the world. This begs the question have we been overcome by the world?

And the second angel sounded, and as it were a great mountain burning with fire was cast into the sea: and the third part of the sea became blood: And the third part of the creatures which were in the sea, and had life, died; and the third part of the ships were destroyed. (Revelation 8:8)

Imagine seeing a mountain of fire being thrown into the sea causing a third part of it to become blood. By parallel, the mountain was on fire when Moses received the Ten Commandments and the rivers turned to blood when God sent a plague upon Egypt. Moses was interceding for the release of the Hebrews from Egyptian slavery. In Exodus 19, we learn the Lord spoke to Moses out of Mount Sinai telling him what he should tell the house of Jacob and the children of Israel. In verses 18–21, we read,

And mount Sinai was altogether on a smoke, because the Lord descended upon it in fire: and the smoke therof ascended as the smoke of a furnace, and the whole mount quaked greatly. And when the voice of the trumpet sounded long and waxed louder and louder, Moses spake, and God answered him by a voice. And the Lord came down upon mount Sinai, on the top of the mount: and the Lord called Moses *up* to the top of the mount: and Moses went up. And the Lord said unto Moses, go down, charge the people, lest they break through unto the Lord to gaze, and many of them perish.

Chapter 20 of Exodus contains the Ten Commandments. In the comparison of Mount Zion to Mount Sinai, we read in Hebrews 12:18–22,

For ye are not come unto the mount that might be touched, and that burned with fire, nor unto blackness, and darkness, and tempest. And the sound of a trumpet and the voice of words: which *voice* they that heard entreated

that the word should not be spoken to them any more:
(For they could not endure that which was commanded,
And if so much as a beast touch the mountain, it shall be
stoned, or thrust through with a dart: And so terrible was
the sight *that* Moses said, I exceedingly fear and quake:)
But ye are come unto mount Zion, and unto the city of the
living God, the heavenly Jerusalem, and to an innumerable
company of angels.

Psalm 46 is full of prophecy as it describes the scenario of the
last days and the peace we can have in the midst of chaos. Verses
1–2 read, "God *is* our refuge and strength, a very present help in
trouble. Therefore will not we fear, though the earth be removed,
and though the mountains be carried into the midst of the sea."
As I imagined the sight of a mountain of fire being thrown into
the sea and the third part of the waters become blood, it occurred
to me it is the blood of Jesus that covers the law. God sent Jesus
to intercede for us to set us free from being slaves to sin. Since
creation, the Lord has been trying to win the hearts of His
people. He sent His prophets to warn His people of impending
judgment but they wouldn't listen. Instead, they turned their
back on their first love to go after the temporal pleasures of idol
worship and pagan rituals. While Moses was receiving the Ten
Commandment, as the mountain burned with fire, the Hebrews
began to worship a golden calf despite having told Moses they
would do what the Lord said.

Once the judgments in Revelation come upon the earth, you
would think man would recognize God and repent. However,
the end of Chapter 9 says that those who were not killed by
the plagues would not repent of the work of their hands that
they should not worship devils and idols of gold, silver, brass,
stone, and wood which could not see hear or walk. Neither did
they repent of their murders, sorceries, fornication, and theft. If
we don't warn people while we have time, think about knowing

that your friends, family, loved ones, even your neighbors or the strangers you see in public, could possibly endure the "Wrath of the Lamb." Every day, we have a choice to touch someone with the love of Jesus. It is the voice of the trumpet that sounded when Moses heard the Lord speak to him from the mountain burning with fire. It is the voice that sounded like a trumpet that John heard while he was on Patmos receiving the visions of Revelation. The second trumpet of this section is in the second series of judgments that come upon the earth to announce the mountain of fire, which gave us the law that is covered by blood as it falls into the sea.

Psalm 46 lets us know the heathen will rage but the Lord will be exalted in the earth. The kingdoms will be removed and the earth will melt at the voice of the Lord. The Lord will make the wars cease and destroy the weapons. The military vehicles He will burn in the fire. For those who trust in the Holy One of Israel, we have these promises found in verses 4, 5, 10, and 11,

> *There* is a river, the streams whereof shall make glad the city of God, the holy *place* of the tabernacles of the most High. God *is* in the midst of her; she shall not be moved: God shall help her, *and that* right early…Be still and know that I *am* God: I will be exalted among the heathen I will be exalted in the earth. The Lord of hosts *is* with us the God of Jacob *is* our refuge. Selah.

BREASTPLATES OF FIRE

> And the sixth angel sounded, and I heard a voice from the four horns of the golden altar which is before God, Saying to the sixth angels which had the trumpet, Loose the four angels which are bound in the great river Euphrates. And the four angels were loosed, which were prepared for an hour, and a day, and a month and a year, for to slay the third part of men. And the number of the army of the

horsemen *were* two hundred thousand thousand: and I heard the number of them. And thus I saw the horses in the vision, and them that sat on them, having breastplates of fire, and of jacinth, and brimstone: and the heads of the horses *were* as the heads of lions; and out of their mouths issued fire and smoke and brimstone. By these three was the third part of men killed, by the fire, and by the smoke, and by the brimstone, which issued out of their mouths. (Revelation 9:13–18)

Chapter 8 ends with: "Woe, woe, woe, to the inhabiters of the earth by reason of the other voices of the trumpet of the three angels, which are yet to sound!" Chapter 9 begins by telling us that John saw a star fall from heaven to earth. This "star" was given the key to the bottomless pit. Once opened, the air is darkened because it is filled with the smoke that came up from the pit. The word for pit used in the Greek could mean a hole in the ground like a well or more likely could mean the abyss, as it would refer to a prison. John describes the creatures that are released as locusts with the power of the earth's scorpions and they are "commanded" not to hurt any green thing but only those who do not have the seal of God in their foreheads. They are told not to kill but only torment them with their sting so much so they will seek death but it will escape them. The shape of these locusts is compared to horses going to battle. They have the face of a man; teeth like a lion, hair like a woman and wear a gold crown. Their breastplates are iron and the sound of their wings is compared to the sound of horses running to battle. We are told a king who is the angel of the bottomless pit rules these creatures. Is the star who opens the bottomless pit this king? John tells us the Hebrew and Greek names for this king. The Hebrew name, Abaddon, is rendered as perishing or Hades. The word abyss and Hades are sometimes used interchangeably, and it is my understanding that it is not a reference to hell. The Greek name, Apollyon, is derived from two words, which could be understood to mean separate from destruction. I submit that this king is not Satan as many have been taught to believe. I am reminded of the "destroying angel" that was stopped in the story of the destruction that ensued in Jerusalem when David numbered the people after a battle. The locusts are commanded to harm those without the seal of God. Abaddon or Apollyon is doing the bidding of the Lord.

The first woe of the fifth trumpet is the destruction that comes up from the earth. The second woe from the sixth trumpet comes as a result of the four angels being released from the Euphrates River. Their onslaught was predetermined to the hour, day, month, and year to kill a third of the men. John heard these four angels have horsemen that are numbered as "two hundred thousand thousand." John's vision of the horsemen describes them wearing breastplates of fire, jacinth, and brimstone. We can imagine fiery breastplates but add to that image the colors of jacinth, which is considered to be a deep blue and of brimstone, which in the Greek language means to have the shape or fashion of flashing yellow sulphur. It is the fire, jacinth, and brimstone that kills the third part of men. However, we are told that their power is in their mouth and tails because their tails were like serpents that had a head and with their tails they hurt. Chapter 9 ends by telling us,

> And the rest of the men which were not killed by these plagues yet repented not of the works of their hands, that they would not worship devils, and idols of gold, and silver, and brass, and stone, and of wood: which neither can see, nor hear, nor walk: Neither repented they of their murders, nor of their sorceries, nor of their fornication, nor of their thefts.

The third woe which comes when the seventh angel's trumpet is recorded in chapter 10 which will be covered in the next section.

While I believe it is essential to our understanding of Revelation to consider what has previously been written about this book, I also know that the Lord through His Holy Spirit wants us to see it with the eyes of understanding that only He can give. Many who try to explain visions have never received a vision from the Lord. Much of what some might consider visions from the Lord these days are the result of a vivid imagination. How can we discern what is true of these things? I am a firm believer in allowing the Word to explain the Word. If we choose to search the Word, we will discover the meaning and receive the understanding. As I study the word, I realize that many with every good intention have been led by their own understanding. The Bible says not to lean on our own understanding and that prophecy is not a result of any private interpretation. So we that desire to learn and understand must constantly evaluate what we see and hear in regard to the Bible. Lord, help us!

FEET AS PILLARS OF FIRE

And I saw another mighty angel come down from heaven clothed with a cloud: and a rainbow *was* upon his head, and his face *was* as it were the sun, and his feet as pillars of fire. (Revelation 10:1)

In Ezekiel, we read a similar description. (See Appearance of Fire in *Fire in the Bible, Genesis-Daniel)* Chapter 1 verses 26–28 read,

And above the firmament that *was* over their heads *was* the likeness of a throne, as the appearance of a sapphire stone: and upon the likeness of the throne *was* the likeness as the appearance of a man above upon it. And I saw as the colour of amber, as the appearance of fire round about within it, from the appearance of his loins even upward, and from the appearance of his loins even downward, I saw as it were the appearance of fire, and it had brightness round about. As the appearance of the bow that is in the cloud in the day of rain, so *was* the appearance of the brightness round about. This *was* the appearance of the likeness of the glory of the Lord. And when I saw *it*, I fell upon my face, and I heard a voice of one that spake.

In verse 24, Ezekiel describes the sound of the wings of the living creatures as sounding like the voice of many waters, which were like the voice of the Almighty.

I remember the very first vision I saw of the Lord. I was in our bedroom, and as I was praying, I saw an altar like a wide pedestal with a baby lamb on it. Around the scene as if it were in the clouds was a rainbow. It was a full circle around the lamb and the altar. The first time I heard the voice of many waters was when I was in my daughter's bedroom. I was praying about worshipping Mary from being raised as a Catholic and I heard that voice say, "There is no such worship in heaven." The first time I heard the still small voice was after listening to the song called "Listen to the Voice" by Leon Patillo in the spring of 1988. I was in my car in my driveway when I first started speaking in tongues and demanded an interpretation from the Lord because I thought I was supposed to know. I then sat on my front porch and that's when I heard the Holy Spirit give me the meaning.

The first vision of fire that I saw was when I left a high school after an assembly that I did with a radio station I worked at. I saw my feet on fire and the Lord reminded me of the scripture in Joshua that says wherever the soles of your feet go that is the land that you claim for me. The most amazing vision was of the Lord in a wall of fire and as I prayed on my face in my bedroom, He said, "If you want to be in my presence, you must go through the fire." I have also seen a vision of fire burning across the map of the United States and one of smoke like a cloud over Tucson.

It is so amazing to me that I have seen the throne of God with a sea of glass before the Ancient of Days. If I read it so many times in the Bible, I could visualize it, but this is a vision. It is not something I imagined. I have also seen the Lord full of fire from head to toe. I see this spiritual fire and it humbles me that God has given me this gift. I remember in the midst of intense pain in the winter of 1996 through the spring of 1997, I would pray and study and write because I could not sleep. I felt as though I went through that wall of fire around the Lord. I also remember almost getting hit by two cars on each side of me and seeing the fire around me as if everything was in slow motion and I knew He sent His angels to protect me that way.

The Baptism of Holy Fire is occurring. I saw it in my husband, John, and I saw it around a close friend and around pastors at a church. I believe God is individually allowing His children to go through the fire to know total reliance on Him, so that when the body of Christ goes through the fire corporately, we will know to rely on Him and Him alone. I know the Lord warned me that John would go through the fire when He would ask me if I would trust Him with John. He did this during my prayer time for almost a year before John had his stroke. He is now asking me to trust Him with my oldest son. I need to release him to the Father's love and discipline.

Some of the other visions I have seen include tongues of fire in the palms of my hand, and the hole in the Lord's hand as He put it in the fountain in heaven and the water ran through His wound. I asked the Lord what the latter vision meant and He said, "My people have not bound up my wounds." When I asked Him what to do, He said, "The acceptable fast," which is found in Isaiah 58.

Another time I saw a vision of an explosion and a shroud over this city and the Lord saying it is not for a time. I remember in Daniel and Revelation about a time, times and a half. In Daniel 7:25, it talks about the dividing of time when the fourth beast will wear out the saints and try to change the times and law. The saints will be given into his hand for a time and times and the dividing of time. And in Daniel 12:7, it tells of the time, times and a half when Satan will have scattered the power of the holy people, when all the end of the wonders that Daniel saw are finished.

Truly, the Lord reveals as we are able to comprehend. Through this study, I am realizing the times of the rapture is three and a half years into the tribulation and I now see that His church Israel will be sealed at that point. This causes these other prophecies to come into play. Those of the tribes of Israel that are sealed in chapter 7 of Revelation recognize Jesus as Messiah after the rapture. Then the Lord sends this church away to be nourished in the wilderness for three and a half years. This wilderness could be what is referred to as the place the daughter of Zion will be protected. The Lord spoke this to me as I drove between Phoenix and Tucson. God is going to do an amazing thing here and I pray to do my part in His perfect time according to His perfect will. I also pray to lay down my desires and dreams if they are not according to His plan.

FIRE FROM THEIR MOUTH

> And I will give *power* unto my two witnesses, and they shall prophesy a thousand two hundred *and* threescore days, (twelve hundred and sixty days or forty-two months; three and one-half years) clothed in sackcloth. These are the two olive trees and the two candlesticks standing before the God of the earth. And if any man will hurt them, fire proceedeth out of their mouth and devoureth their enemies: and if any man will hurt them, he must in this manner be killed. (Revelation 11:3–5)

There is a reference to the two anointed ones in the fourth chapter of Zechariah. In this chapter, Zechariah asks the angel who are the two olive trees which give an endless supply of oil to the bowl on top of the candlestick which has seven lamps on it. First, the angel says that it is the word of the Lord to Zerubbabel saying, "Not by might, nor by power, but by My Spirit says the

Lord." The second time in verse 11 there is no response, so we read Zechariah asks him a second time in verse 12, which is really the third time altogether. The angel asks Zechariah if he knows who they are and he answers no.

Some teach they are Enoch and Elijah. In the *Amplified Bible*, the footnote says these are the two sons of oil, Joshua the high priest and Zerubbabel the prince of Judah, the two anointed ones who stand before the Lord of the whole earth as His anointed instruments. I am not sure of this either. Zerubbabel was with Joshua and led the return of exiles from Babylon and started the rebuilding of the temple. The Lord declares that Zerubbabel will finish the temple.

I appreciate this insight from Matthew Henry's Commentary found on Biblos.com regarding the two witnesses:

> How they were supported and supplied during the discharge of their great and hard work: they stood before the God of the whole earth, and he gave them power to prophesy. He made them to be like Zerubbabel and Joshua, the two olive trees and candlestick in the vision of Zechariah 4:2, etc. God gave them the oil of holy zeal, and courage, and strength, and comfort; he made them olive trees, and their lamps of profession were kept burning by the oil of inward gracious principles, which they received from God. They had oil not only in their lamps, but in their vessels-habits of spiritual life, light, and zeal.

In Zechariah 3:8, the angel showed him that Joshua was standing before the angel of the Lord and then the Lord of host tells Joshua that he will bring forth His servant the Branch. In Zechariah 6:12, it says, "Thus speaketh the Lord of hosts, saying, Behold the man whose name is The BRANCH: and he shall grow up out of his place, and he shall build the temple of the Lord." In Jeremiah 23:5, it says the Lord will raise unto David a righteous Branch, and a King shall reign and prosper, and shall execute judgment and justice in the earth. Jeremiah 33:14–16 repeats this promise,

> Behold, the days come, saith the Lord, that I will perform that good thing which I have promised unto the house of Israel and to the house of Judah. In those days, and at that time, will I cause the Branch of righteousness to grow up unto David; and he shall execute judgment and righteousness in the land. In those days shall Judah be saved, and Jerusalem shall dwell safely: and this *is the name* wherewith she shall be called, The Lord our righteousness.

In Isaiah 4:2, it describes how the branch of the Lord will be beautiful and the fruit of earth will be excellent for those that escape Israel. In verse 4, it says the Lord will wash away the filth of the daughters of Zion and purge the blood in the midst of Jerusalem by the spirit of judgment and by the spirit of burning. Once He has done this, those that are left in Zion and Jerusalem will be called holy, that is everyone that is written among the living in Jerusalem. In verse 5, the Lord will create over every dwelling place a cloud and smoke by day and the shining of a flaming fire by night; for upon all the glory shall be a defense.

Why does the Lord enable these two anointed ones to have fire come out of their mouths? Is this the "spirit of burning" referred to in the above paragraph? Is this purging that will take place as these two witnesses prophecy meant to cleanse the people, the land, or both? The presentation of the two witnesses comes as a result of the sixth angel sounding the sixth trumpet. It is the second woe of three warned of at the end of chapter 8. Further on in Revelation 10:7 we read, "But in the days of the voice of the seventh angel, when he shall begin to sound, the mystery of God should be finished, as he hath declared to his servants the prophets." What's interesting is that John is told that he must prophesy again to many peoples, and nations, and tongues, and kings at the end of chapter 10. Sometimes, I wonder if John could be one of the two witnesses. What I love about studying the word, even just typing it verbatim, I end up seeing things I never saw before. Revelation 11:15 lets us know that the kingdoms of this world become the kingdoms of "our Lord and of his Christ and he shall reign for ever and ever."

What is the main purpose of these two witnesses? Revelation 11:6–7 says they can "shut the heavens" to prevent rain for as long as they prophecy. They also can turn water to blood and cause all kinds of plagues. It isn't until they have finished their testimony that the beast from the bottomless pit kills them. This is not the same as the angel of the bottomless pit named Abaddon or Apollyon. Their death is a cause for gift-giving and rejoicing while their bodies remain in the street for three and a half days until the "spirit of life from God" enters them and they stand on their feet. "Great fear" overcomes all who see this as they hear a "great voice from heaven" calling them up to heaven in a cloud. An earthquake follows that kills seven thousand and the remnant give God glory.

What happens to this remnant? Verse 18 reads,

> And the nations were angry, and thy wrath is come, and the time of the dead, *that* they should be judged, and that thou shouldest give reward unto thy servants the prophets, and to the saints, and them that fear thy name, small and great: and shouldest destroy them which destroy the earth.

John is fluctuating between visions of heaven and earth as this revelation takes place because the last verse of chapter 11 says that the temple of God was opened and he could see the ark of the testament. He also saw and heard lightnings, thunderings, voices, hail, and an earthquake. Interestingly, John is told to measure the temple at the beginning of this chapter, and at the end of the chapter, we are told he sees the temple in heaven. Of course, the chapter divisions were not in the original text but John is given a juxtaposition of the two temples. More than anything else, I have to wonder what is the testimony of these two witnesses. Does the fire that comes from their mouth represent their prophecies?

Prophets speak of God's impending judgment and warn so that the people might repent. There is the remnant that glorifies God as a result of the ascension of the two witnesses. Within this chapter is the designation of the time of judgment. Their voices will be heard during a time that resembles the challenges that the Egyptian pharaoh faced as Moses attempted to make him release the Hebrews. At the time of the testimony of the two witnesses there is a temple on earth but the Gentiles are not included in the measurements made by John. Who is worshipping in this temple during this three-and-a-half-year time frame? Is it the Jews that were sealed? Why is the beast from the bottomless pit allowed to kill them? The more I pour over this book, the more questions I have.

Once again, I refer to Matthew Henry's commentary on this book, I quote,

The slaying of the witnesses. To make their testimony more strong, they must seal it with their blood. Here observe,

1. The time when they should be killed: When they have finished their testimony. They are immortal; they are invulnerable, till their work be done. Some think it ought to be rendered, when they were about to finish their testimony. When they had prophesied in sackcloth the greatest part of the 1260 years, then they should feel the last effect of antichristian malice.

2. The enemy that should overcome and slay them- the beast that ascendeth out of the bottomless pit. Antichrist, the great instrument of the devil, should make war against them, not only with the arms of subtle and sophistical learning, but chiefly with open force and violence; and God would

permit his enemies to prevail against his witnesses for a time.

3. The barbarous usage of these slain witnesses; the malice of their enemies was not satiated with their blood and death, but pursued even their dead bodies. (a) They would not allow them a quiet grave; their bodies were cast out in the open street, the high street of Babylon, or in the high road leading to the city. This city is spiritually called Sodom for monstrous wickedness, and Egypt for idolatry and tyranny; and here Christ in his mystical body has suffered more than in any place in the world. (b) Their dead bodies were insulted by the inhabitants of the earth, and their death was a matter of mirth and joy to the antichristian world, v. 10. They were glad to be rid of these witnesses, who by their doctrine and example had teased, terrified, and tormented the consciences of their enemies; these spiritual weapons cut wicked men to the heart, and fill them with the greatest rage and malice against the faithful.

Within this commentary, Henry uses the time frame of 1260 years. I believe it should be days. The most striking comment he makes regarding this passage is that these witnesses prophesy during the "time of treading down" and that they wear sackcloth, which is a sign of affliction and sorrow for the abominations committed. He writes there is "abundant cause to prophesy in sackcloth" for the state of religion.

Even during such a time of blatant rejection of the truth of God's word, the Lord's hand is still stretched out to convert souls. He uses these prophets to testify of the truth. The truth so powerful as when Jeremiah prophesied and the Lord told him

His word would be like "fire in his mouth." Does the word of God burn so brightly in our hearts that out of its abundance a fire will burn to expose the darkness in our world? Do our words burn so brightly that they will enlighten the listener to know the One who is the word of God? The answer is only if our words are His words.

FALSE FIRE

> And he doeth great wonders, so that he maketh fire come down from heaven on the earth in the sight of men. (Rev. 13:13)

In this chapter, we read of the beast coming out of the sea, the dragon who I see as another reference to that beast and another beast that looked like a lamb but spoke as a dragon. It is the second beast that is referred to in the thirteenth verse that deceives those that dwell on the earth not only by his appearance but by the miracles he is able to do in the "sight of the first beast." The first beast was the one who came back to life after receiving a deadly wound on one of his heads. The second beast has the power to make those that dwell on earth create an image of the first beast. This second beast has the power to give life to the image and make it speak. The second beast also uses his power to cause those that won't worship the image of the first beast to be killed. The second beast also causes all "small and great, rich and poor, free and bond" to receive a mark in order to buy or sell. Verse 17 reads, "And that no man might buy or sell, save he that had the mark, or the name of the beast, or the number of his name." While many look to the number 666 as the mark, notice that it says the mark *or* the name of the beast *or* the number. It is the dragon/first beast that gives the second beast his power according to verse 4 where we also learn that this dragon is also worshipped.

I was struck by the reality of images being brought to life in the entertainment industry after watching the movie *Avatar*. The *Encarta World English Dictionary* gives this definition for avatar: 1. An incarnation of a Hindu deity in human or animal form, especially of the incarnations of Vishnu such as Rama and Krishna. 2. Somebody who embodies, personifies, or is the manifestation of an idea or concept. 3. A movable three-dimensional image that can be used to represent somebody in cyberspace, for example, an Internet user. I personally didn't want to watch the movie but after I learned that my young grandson was taken to see it at a birthday party I wanted to know what he was exposed to.

The phrase "power to give life to the image of the beast" came to mind as I considered how the digital artwork creates such life like creatures. I am acutely aware of how the enemy subtly conditions us to accept these demonic images as good. The Bible warns of the day when good is called evil and evil is called good. I pray mercy for all that young children are exposed to in the form of entertainment. Most families considers whatever Disney produces as safe when from the beginning it has been promoted as the Magic Kingdom. Digital imagery is now 3D and 4D and gives lifelike dimension to what is being viewed on the screen. It is modern day magic! The Old Testament warns against magic in all its forms: divination, sorcery, necromancy (consulting the dead), astrology, and consulting mediums now called psychics. Once while dusting my TV, I realized that the singular form of the word media is medium. I'm not saying that everything that's in the media is comparable to consulting a medium but you have to admit the power it has over our lives and how most people in our culture would never go without some form of media in the background.

In regard to digital imagery, realize the means by which digital information is stored in computers came about as a result of the use of the binary system. Different than the decimal system based on ten digits, the binary system is based on two digits:

zero and one. I woke in the middle of the night realizing that is why Revelation 13:17 tells us about the "number of his name." The alphabet must be converted to its numerical equivalent for processing in the computer. I wonder what the binary equivalent of the number 666 is? Beyond that, could that binary equivalent be reconverted alphabetically? Online research acknowledged a man named Lebniz born in of all years, 1666, to have first concluded that verbal ideas could be converted to numbers. The final verse of Revelation 13 says, "Here is wisdom. Let him that hath understanding count the number of the beast for it is the number of a man; and his number *is* Six hundred threescore *and* six."

On another level, we need to understand how biometrics could be the means by which many will receive the mark of the beast. Biometric technology converts biological characteristics to numerical equivalents for processing in computers as well. The UPC label on every product we buy uses the binary system for scanning at the register. I heard on the radio that these labels are being replaced by RFID (Radio Frequency Identification Devices). This means the positions of these items could be traced to your home. You will notice these small raised plastic devices glued inside of boxes and flat circuitry made into cloth-covered labels on garments.

The conditioning once again is for convenience. Eventually, there will be no need for checkout lanes since these RFID will be scanned when you leave the store and the price will be automatically deducted from your checking account. Can you imagine every item of produce being implanted with an RFID? Why would that be necessary? It's all about control. Imagine your employer has subscribed to the federally mandated health care program and has a vested interest in your health. Since all our medical records are also being sent to a federal database, we could see more control by the federal government and/or employers as to what products we can or cannot buy.

Just as animals are being "chipped" with the RFID to help locate them if they are lost or stolen, now there is a push to have children *marked* with these chips in the event of kidnapping. My last two grandchildren had an RFID on the umbilical cord clamp so babies cannot be taken from the hospital without an alarm being set off. Another application of these devices would be for all our medical information to be placed on a chip and implanted in our hand or forehead, which is considered the best location. I even believe the increase in the number of tattoos is another form of conditioning that will eventually lead to the acceptance of the mark of the beast.

Even more bizarre is the effect that genetically modified organisms are having on the agricultural community. The seeds of these plants do not germinate so the farmers have to go back to the giant agricultural conglomerates for seeds to plant their crops. How horribly strange it is that cloned animals cannot reproduce as well. Man without God believes the lie from the garden… that he could be like God. Satan would have him believe that he can create life. We cannot even fathom the disastrous results of the genetic experiments that are being done. Sometimes I think this will result in human mutations resembling beasts and so that explains the conditioning to accept the creatures in movies as normal.

Allow me just one more tangent. Searching the Hebrew and Greek root words is fascinating. The word used to refer to Satan in the garden is serpent. The Hebrew word for a serpent or snake means to hiss or whisper a magic spell, to prognosticate or use enchantments. The word for sorcerer in the Greek means to whisper a spell, enchant or use a spell or witchcraft. The word for enchantments means to blaze, enwrapping magic or flaming. The root of that word means to lick, to blaze, to burn, to set on fire or kindle. (Refer to the Introduction at the beginning of the book for another tangent on fire.) This explains why the second beast using the power also referred to as energy of the first beast is able to cause fire to come from heaven to deceive those that live on the earth. Furthermore, when we read that Satan beguiled Eve in the garden, the word beguiled in the Hebrew means to lead astray, mentally delude, morally seduce, greatly and utterly, according to the Strong's Concordance. Even electricity must have seemed to be magic when it was first invented. An inventor named Tesla, born in the mid-1800s, is credited online to have created man-made lightning.

In the definition for magician in my *Bible Dictionary* that was printed over one hundred years ago, I learned the Egyptian magicians that came against Moses were "two in number." That struck me when I thought of how the binary code uses only two numbers. According to 2 Timothy 3:8, the names of the two were Jannes and Jambres. The root word for magician in the Greek is Magoi or Magi. The Magi that brought gifts to Jesus at his birth were from a Persian sect. They originally were recognized as a priestly caste as one of the six tribes of Medes who continued to influence the Persians during the time of Cyrus. They worshipped the elements: fire, earth, air, and water. They had fire temples and kept them burning continually. We are told that Daniel the prophet prospered during the reigns of Darius the Mede and Cyrus the Persian. Thanks to the historical research formulated in novel form in the *A.D. Chronicles* by my favorite authors, Brock and Bodie Thoene. I learned the Hebrew understanding of astronomy influenced the Persians and that is how the wise men came to follow stars that told of the king that was born in Bethlehem. In Daniel 6:25, Darius, King of the Medes decreed that all of his kingdom should tremble and fear before the God of Daniel who is the living God whose dominion would last even until the end.

It is so like Satan to counterfeit and imitate. There is an unholy trinity of sorts in Revelation 13 as we read about the dragon, the beast, and the image of the beast just as we have Holy Trinity of God the Father, God the Son, and God the Holy Spirit. He imitates God by using signs, wonders, and miracles, even fire from heaven. To discern the counterfeit, we need to know the real one. We can know the only true living God by spending time in the word studying the Bible. John 1 tells us that the word became flesh in the person of Jesus Christ and He wants to reveal Himself to us through His Holy Spirit.

TORMENTED BY FIRE AND BRIMSTONE

> And the third angel followed them, saying with a loud voice, If any man worship the beast and his image, and receive his mark in his forehead, or in his hand, The same shall drink of the wine of the wrath of God, which is poured out without mixture into the cup of his indignation; and he shall be tormented with fire and brimstone in the presence of the holy angels, and in the presence of the Lamb: And the smoke of their torment ascendeth up forever an ever; and they have no rest day nor night, who worship the beast and his image, and whosoever receiveth the mark of his name. Here is the patience of the saints: here are they that keepeth the commandment of God and the faith of Jesus. (Revelation 14:9–12)

This chapter begins with John seeing the Lamb on Mt. Zion with the 144,000 who had "his Father's name in their forehead," who were singing a new song having been redeemed from the earth and who follow the Lamb wherever He goes. The end of the chapter describes the one like the Son of man upon a cloud wearing a golden crown and carrying a sharp sickle who comes to reap the harvest of the earth. In between, we read of those who are tormented by fire and brimstone because they worshipped the beast and his image and received his mark. Before we learn of this torment, we hear of an angel flying in the midst of heaven who preaches the everlasting gospel to all who dwell on the earth. According to verse 7, the warning goes out: "Fear God and give glory to him; for the hour of his judgment is come: and worship him that made heaven and earth, and the sea, and the fountains of waters." Another angel tells that Babylon is fallen because she made all nations drink of the wine of the wrath of her fornication. After this, we learn of those who received the mark and worshipped the beast, since they ignored the warning of the angel who preached the everlasting gospel, we read of what the voice from heaven says in verse 13. It reads, "Blessed *are* the dead which die in the Lord from henceforth: Yea, saith the Spirit, that they may rest from their labours; and their works do follow them."

It's incredulous to think that after an angel from heaven covers the earth with the announcement of the message to worship God that there are still those who chose to worship the beast and his image instead and receive his mark. The one driving force behind their decisions is their overwhelming need to buy and sell. So that explains the patience of the saints who keep the commandments of God and faith of Jesus. The first commandment forbids any other gods and by having faith in Jesus these saints know the Lord will provide.

It seems our nation is being tested as our economy falters and so many have lost jobs. How will we learn to trust the Lord if we have to make it through part of the tribulation if we cannot trust Him to provide now? Having faith in Jesus means to believe Him when He said our Father in heaven will meet our needs. There's a big difference between wants and needs and times like these make us realize what's really important. The overabundance in our culture is sad. Why is it necessary to have one aisle in the grocery devoted to cereal? How many clothes do we really need anyway? Ever since my husband and I started living in our travel trailer, we've learned how little we really need. Life is so much simpler and the Lord has been able to prove His loving care for us.

I don't believe our economy will recover because I can see how we are gradually being forced into a global economy. It may evolve out of a North American Union that does away with our currency and Constitution. It's only a matter of time before America, as we know it ceases to exist. It is a necessary step to begin the prophetic cycle that will usher in the millennial reign of Christ. Of course, no one wants to consider the possibility of going through part of the tribulation or being martyred for believing in Jesus, but there will be no peace until the Lord reigns on earth as He does in heaven.

THE ANGEL WITH POWER OVER FIRE

And I heard a voice from heaven saying unto me, Write, Blessed *are* the dead which die in the Lord from henceforth: Yea, saith the Spirit, that they may rest from their labours; and their works do follow them. And I looked and behold a white cloud, and upon the cloud *one* sat like unto the Son of man, having on his head a golden crown, and in his hand a sharp sickle. And another angel came out of the temple, crying with a loud voice to him that sat on the cloud, Thrust in thy sickle, and reap: for the time is come for thee to reap; for the harvest of the earth is ripe. And he that sat on the cloud thrust in his sickle on the earth: and the earth was reaped. And another angel came out of the temple which is in heaven, he also having a sharp sickle. And another angel came out from the altar, which had power over fire; and cried with a loud cry to him that had the sharp sickle, saying, Thrust in thy sharp sickle, and gather the clusters of the vine of the earth; for her grapes are fully ripe. And the angel thrust in his sickle into the earth, and gathered the vine of the earth, and cast it into the great winepress of the wrath of God. And the winepress was trodden without the city, and blood came out of the winepress, even unto the horse bridles, by the space of a thousand and six hundred furlongs. (Revelation 14:13–20)

There are two different harvests mentioned here. One is for the reaping of the ripe harvest on earth and the second is for the gathering of the clusters of the vine of earth. The grapes of the vine are put in the great winepress for the wrath of God. The first angel cries out with a loud voice to the Son of man on the cloud to use the sharp sickle for the reaping of the earth. The third angel who is described as the one who came out of the altar and has power over fire tells the second angel to put in his sharp sickle for the gathering of the clusters of grapes. In Joel 3:13, in the valley of Jehoshaphat, the sickle is put in for the harvest is ripe and that is where God will judge all the heathen. It says that to get down because the press is full, and the vats overflow because the wickedness is great.

In Revelation 14:18, we learn of the angel with power over fire. In Revelation 7:1, we read of the angels that hold back the wind. In Revelation 16:5, we read of the angel of the water. Here we learn of the angels that control three of the four elements, but which angel has power on earth? Revelation 12:9 reads, "And the great dragon was cast out, that old serpent, called the Devil and Satan, which deceiveth the whole world: he was cast out into the earth and his angels were cast out with him." Furthermore, verse 12 reads, "Therefore rejoice, *ye* heavens and ye that dwell in them. Woe to the inhabiters of earth and of the sea! for the devil is come down unto you, having great wrath." The angel with power over fire came out from the altar of the temple in heaven. Jude 1:6 reads, "And the angels which kept not their first estate, but left their own habitation, he hath reserved in everlasting chains under darkness unto the judgment of the great day."

From Genesis 3, we know that the serpent was in the garden of Eden. His rebellion destroyed the perfect harmony of the four elements of creation. This helps to understand why 2 Peter 3:10 says,

> But the day of the Lord will come as a thief in the night; in the which the heavens shall pass away with a great noise, and the elements shall melt with fervent heat, the earth also and the works therein shall be burned up.

Our hope is found in verse 13, which reads, "Nevertheless we, according to his promise, look for new heavens and new earth, wherein dwelleth righteousness."

A SEA OF GLASS MINGLED WITH FIRE

> And I saw as it were a sea of glass mingled with fire: and them that had gotten the victory over the beast, and over his image, and over his mark, *and* over the number of his name, stand on the sea of glass, having the harps of God. (Revelation 15:2)

John the Revelator saw seven angles with the seven plagues representing the fullness of God's wrath. In the seventh verse of this chapter, it says that one of the four beasts, also known as the living creatures, gave the seven angels the seven vials or bowls full of God's wrath. In verse 8, it tells us that the temple was filled with smoke from the glory of God and His power so that no man could enter until the plagues were fulfilled. In verse 3, it says that those that were playing the harps sang the song of Moses.

Exodus 15:1–3 reads,

> Then sang Moses and the children of Israel this song unto the Lord, and spake, saying, I will sing unto the Lord, for he has triumphed gloriously: the horse and his rider hath he thrown into the sea. The Lord is my strength and song, and he is become my salvation: he is my God, and I will

prepare him an habitation; my father's God and I will exalt him. The Lord is a man of war; the Lord is his name.

Those that stand victorious endured the first half of the tribulation and were willing to die for their faith in Jesus and resisted bowing down to the beast and his image and refused to receive his mark or the number of his name.

Try to imagine this sight in Revelation 15. In essence, they stand on the fire-laden sea of glass. This event precedes the opening of "the temple of the tabernacle of the testimonies in heaven." Our minds cannot fathom the power and intensity of those testimonies. So powerful are these testimonies that God's glory and his power filled the temple with smoke so that no one could enter the temple until the seven angels pour out their vials/bowls.

What is the relation between those standing on the sea of glass mingled with fire to the temple of testimonies? Those who overcome testify in verses 3–4:

> Great and marvelous *are* thy works, Lord God Almighty, just and true *are* thy ways, thou King of saints. Who shall not fear thee, O Lord, and glorify thy name? for *thou* only *art* holy: for all nations shall come and worship before thee; for thy judgments are made manifest.

The great voice that speaks out of the temple says to the seven angels in the first verse of chapter 16: "Go your ways, and pour out the vials of wrath of God upon the earth." This voice testifies of judgment and wrath. Revelation 16:7 reads, "And I heard another out of the altar say, Even so, Lord God Almighty, true and righteous *are* thy judgments." The great voice speaks again from the temple in heaven in verse 17 saying, "It is done."

The judgment for our sins was covered by Jesus when He died on the cross and He said those same words, "It is done." There is no need for any to suffer the wrath of God! Yet, there are those that refuse to believe that Jesus could stand in their place so they have condemned themselves to the true and righteous judgment of God's wrath. During the first half of the tribulation, they chose to bow down to the beast and his image and receive his mark. If only they would have listened to the words found in 2 Peter 3:7 and 9, "But the heavens and the earth which are now, by the same word are kept in store, reserved unto fire against the day of judgment and perdition of ungodly men." But the Lord is "not willing that any should perish, but that all should come to repentance. Those who refuse the redemption offered by Christ will suffer in the lake of fire but those who refuse to worship the beast and his image and do not receive his mark will stand and sing victoriously in the fire of the sea of glass. They overcame by the word of their testimony and were willing to lay down their lives for Jesus just as He did for them.

SCORCHED WITH FIRE

And the fourth angel poured out his vial upon the sun; and power was given unto him to scorch men with fire. And men were scorched with great heat, and blasphemed the name of God, which hath power over these plagues: and they repented not to give him glory. (Revelation 16:8–9)

The first of the seven vials caused all who had the mark of the beast to have terrible sores. The second vial caused the sea to turn into blood like that of a dead man. The third vial turned the waters to blood. The same kind of plague happened in Exodus, and is written of in the Psalms. In Psalm 79:1–3, it talks about the heathen and how they shed the blood of God's servants like water around Jerusalem. In verses 6 and 7 of Revelation 16, it says that God has given them blood to drink because they deserve it and God's judgments are true and righteous. Psalm 119:137 repeats that God's judgments are righteous and upright.

In Exodus 10:21, the people told Moses to stretch his hand toward the heavens that there may be darkness over the land. The fifth angel's vial that follows the scorching fire was poured out on the seat of the beast and brought darkness and excruciating pain to his kingdom. The sixth angel dries up the Euphrates River to make a way for the kings of the east. In Isaiah 11:16, it tells us of the highway for the remnant left in Assyria as it was to Israel in the day that he came up out of the land of Egypt.

In 1 Kings 22:21–22, we are told of a spirit that stood before the Lord that will be a lying spirit in the mouth of the prophets just as there is in Revelation 16:13. It refers to these loathsome spirits as frogs leaping from the mouth of the dragon, beast, and false prophet just as there was a plague of frogs in Exodus 8:7 where the magicians by their enchantments brought up the frogs on the land of Egypt. The kings of the earth are gathered at Armageddon before the seventh vial is poured out. The great voice saying, "It is done," precedes the voices, thunders, and lightnings of the last vial. The earthquake that is spoken of in Revelation 16:18 is said to be unlike any that has been since men have dwelt on the earth.

Revelation 16:21 tells of the great hailstones and how men blasphemed God for this plague. Exodus 9:23–24 says,

> And Moses stretched forth his rod toward heaven: and the Lord sent thunder and hail, and the fire ran along upon the ground; and the Lord rained hail upon the land of Egypt. So there was hail, and fire mingled with the hail, very grievous, such as there was none like it in all the land of Egypt since it became a nation.

Revelation 16 concludes with the great city being divided into three parts. The cities of the nations fell and God remembered Babylon to give her the "cup of the wine of the fierceness of his wrath." Despite all these plagues men still blasphemed God.

Why would there be so many parallels to the plagues when Moses delivered the Hebrews from slavery with the plagues from the seven vials in Revelation? God in His righteous judgments is bringing a final deliverance from the slavery to the one world system instituted by the antichrist. Truly, the Lord is letting His people go from the bondage of death into the promised land of eternal life in His presence.

THE WHORE AND WOMAN BURNED WITH FIRE

And he saith unto me, The waters which thou sawest, where the whore sitteth, are peoples, and multitudes, and nations, and tongues. And the ten horns which thou sawest upon the beast, these shall hate the whore, and shall make her desolate and naked, and shall eat her flesh, and burn her with fire. For God hath put in their hearts to fulfill his will and to agree and give their kingdom unto the beast, until the words of God be fulfilled…Therefore shall her (Babylon's) plagues come in one day, death and mourning, and famine; and she shall be utterly burned with fire: for strong is the Lord God who judgeth her. (Revelation 17:15–17; 18:8)

The last verse of chapter 17 tells us the whore is the great city that rules over the kings of the earth. First, the kings of the earth burn the whore but in chapter 18 it is God that destroys Babylon by fire. There is a distinction between the two. The whore is the great city that prostitutes itself for Babylon. The whore upon many waters is sitting on a red beast with seven heads and ten horns. The ten horns or ten kings have no kingdom but have power for an hour. They have one mind and give their power to the beast that was, is not, and yet is. This is the eighth king, the one that goes into perdition.

These kings make war with the Lamb, but the Lamb overcomes them because He is the King of kings and Lord of lords. The waters are many peoples. The seven heads are seven mountains.

Babylon is the great city, which reigns over the kings of the earth. In her was found the blood of prophets and of the saints that were slain on the earth. In Revelation 18, she is destroyed in one hour and utterly burned with fire and the merchants stand afar off and weep and mourn over her because no man buys their merchandise anymore, which includes the souls of men. The merchants of these things, which were made rich by her, shall stand afar off for the fear of her torment, weeping and wailing.

A mighty angel takes the millstone and throws it into the sea saying, "with violence shall the great city Babylon be thrown down and shall be found no more." The mighty angel says that Babylon has fallen and that the kings of the earth that committed fornication with her are rich because of her delicacies. Then there is no music, no craftsmen, and no sound of the millstone, no voice of the bridegroom or bride. The merchants were the great men of the earth who were deceived by her sorceries.

Revelation 18:4 intrigues me because it reads, "And I heard another voice from heaven, saying, Come out of her my people, that ye be not partakers of her sins, and that ye receive not her plagues." This would have to be the final remnant that makes it through the second half of the tribulation.

Could the United States be the whore that prostitutes herself for the sake of Babylon? This nation imports so much. We are like the many waters because of all the nations that have come here. Destruction could come from the kings of the earth because they will operate as "with one mind." When I saw the vision of a fire spreading across the United States beginning in Tucson, I never asked the Lord what it meant. I wanted it to be the fire of the Holy Spirit spreading across this nation. But what if the Lord was showing me the fire that will burn this nation because of our harlotry for Babylon. There will come a time when the kings of the earth will come against the whore and burn her with fire because Revelation 17:17 tells us God will put it in their hearts to fulfill his will. There will also come a time when Babylon will be destroyed by God's fire because Revelation 18:8 tells us she will "utterly be burned with fire."

THE LAKE OF FIRE

And I saw an angel standing in the sun; and he cried with a loud voice, saying to all the fowls that fly in the midst of heaven, Come and gather yourselves together unto the supper of the great God; That ye may eat the flesh of kings, and the flesh of captains, and the flesh of mighty men, and the flesh of horses, and of them that sit on them, and the flesh of all men, *both* free and bond, both small and great. And I saw the beast, and the kings of the earth, and their armies, gathered together to make war against him that sat on the horse, and against his army. And the beast was taken, and with him the false prophet that wrought miracles before him, with which he deceived them that had received the mark of the beast, and them that worshipped his image. These both were cast alive into a lake of fire burning with brimstone. And the remnant were slain with the *sword* of him that sat upon the horse, which sword proceeded out of his mouth: and all the fowls were filled with their flesh…And the devil that deceived them was cast into the lake of fire and brimstone, where the beast and the false prophet *are*, and shall be tormented day and night forever and ever…And death and hell were cast into the lake of fire. This is the second death. And whosoever was not found written in the book of life was cast into the lake of fire…But the fearful, and unbelieving, and the abominable, and murderers and whoremongers, and sorcerers, and idolaters, and all liars, shall have their part in the lake which burneth with fire and brimstone: which is the second death. (Revelation 19:17–21; 20:10, 14–15; 21:8)

Chapter 19 begins with the Alleluias to God in heaven by the "great voice" of a multitude because the great whore had been destroyed for shedding the blood of the Lord's servants. Then the "voice of many waters" announces that the time for the marriage of the Lamb had come because the bride was ready. Her clean and white garment is called the "righteousness of the saints" in verses 7 to 8. In the following verses, the heavens are opened to reveal the one called Faithful and True, with eyes like flames of fire wearing many crowns sitting on a white horse, who judges and makes war in righteousness. His clothing is dipped in blood and His name is called, "The Word of God" which is the sword that comes out of His mouth. The armies of heaven wearing white on white horses follow Him. He comes to rule the nations with a rod of iron and to tread the "winepress of the fierceness and wrath of Almighty God."

It is Jesus, the King of kings and Lord of lords, who comes upon the white horse to slay the wicked with His sword. The invitation goes out for the "supper of the great God" to eat the slain flesh of those who followed the beast and his armies but notice the beast and false prophet are "cast alive" into the lake of fire. In a commentary by Wesley, he made the opposite observation by stating that Enoch and Elijah went to heaven alive. The beast and false prophet are cast into the lake of fire before the millennium. The devil is bound for a thousand years and then is cast into the lake of fire after the millennium.

The lake of fire is not hell because hell and death are cast into the lake of fire according to Revelation 20:14. Twice we read that the lake of fire is considered the second death. By contrast, a second birth occurs for all who are born again by receiving Jesus as Lord and Savior. These are the ones whose names are written in the Lamb's Book of Life. In Revelation 20:4–6, those who were beheaded for not receiving the mark of the beast or worshipping him are called the first resurrection. They will be priest of God and of Christ during the millennium. The second death has no power over them. The rest of the dead will not live again until after the millennium.

Revelation 20:12–13 reads,

> And I saw the dead, small and great, stand before God; and the books were opened: and another book was opened, which *is the book* of life; and the dead were judged out of those things written in the books, according to their works. And the sea gave up the dead which were in it; and death and hell delivered up the dead which were in them: and they were judged every man according to their works.

The phrase "death and hell delivered up the dead which were in them" stands out because we read in Revelation1:18 that Jesus says that he holds the keys to hell and death. The end result is that hell and death are destroyed for all eternity in the lake of fire along with the unholy triad and those who rejected Jesus.

Revelation 21:8 lists those who goes into the lake of fire as the fearful, unbelieving, abominable, murderers, whoremongers, sorcerers, idolaters, and liars. The "fearful" seem to be out of place in this list except for the fact that they don't know the perfect love that gets rid of fear. Jesus is perfect love and we all need to know Jesus to know His perfect love. To know His perfect love is to know that our names are written in His Book of Life. To have our names written in His Book of Life means we don't need to have any fear of the lake of fire.

THE FINAL FIRE

> And they went up on the breadth of the earth, and compassed the camp of the saints about, and the beloved city: and fire came down from God out of heaven and devoured them. (Revelation 20:9)

This judgment comes after the millennium and before the final judgment. Satan is released from the bottomless pit for a season and goes out to the four quarters of the earth to deceive and to gather together to battle all those whose numbers were as the sands of the sea. This is after a thousand years of peace as Jesus reigned on earth from Jerusalem. I am certain those who were martyred during the last half of the tribulation live and reign with Jesus for a thousand years, but I wonder if all those born during the millennium live a thousand years. In the mid-nineties, when my husband and I were at a Christian concert watching young people praise the Lord, I heard the Lord say, "This is the generation that will usher in the millennium." It fascinates me to think of who will inhabit the earth during that blessed time. With all the wars and rumors of wars that we hear about today, how wonderful to imagine Jesus ruling the earth in peace. Yet, how can it be that Satan could once again be able to deceive so many from all over the world to come against the saints and the beloved city? My only answer would have to be that the Lord still gives His creation free will.

Fire come downs from God out of heaven to devour all that surround the camp of the saints and the beloved city. Then the devil is thrown into the lake of fire where the false prophet and the beast are to be tormented forever and ever. Once this happens, the judgment books are opened and all the dead stand before God at the great white throne. All those whose names are not in the Lamb's Book of Life are thrown into the lake of fire, which is called the second death. Revelation 20:6 reads, "Blessed and holy is he that hath part in the first resurrection: on such the second death hath no power, but they shall be priests of God and of Christ, and shall reign with him a thousand years." God's judgment in the lake of fire is just and righteous and motivated by His love for His Bride. No longer will the enemy of our souls be able to deceive. He receives eternal torment for the torment he inflicted down through the ages. The beast and false prophets as his agents receive the same punishment. All who reject eternal life through Jesus condemned themselves and will follow Satan to the lake of fire.

I grieve wondering how to prevent the kind of deception from the father of lies that would sentence anyone to eternity apart from the presence of God the Father, Son, and Holy Spirit. While there is still time, the love of God must be shared. While there is still time, the truth of Jesus, the Word of God needs to be told. While there is still time, Satan needs to be exposed for who he is and what eternity with him really means. So many are following false prophets and doctrines that demons teach. In the name of tolerance and coexistence, the infallible Word of God is being compromised and even dismissed. We are living in the day when so many have their own designer god. A god of their own creation, an idol that stands in front of the face of the One True Living God. God is not willing that any should perish but that all should could have eternal life…not the second death in the lake of fire.

Our hope and promise is found in Revelation 21 where it tells us of the first heaven and earth passing away but also of a new heaven and earth to be created. The New Jerusalem, the holy city, will come down from God out of heaven as a bride prepared for her husband. The great voice out of heaven says that the tabernacle of God is with men and He will dwell with them and they shall be his people and God Himself shall be with them, and be their God.

THE ETERNAL FLAME

King James Version: Set me as a seal upon thine heart, as a seal upon thine arm: for love *is* strong as death; jealousy *is* cruel as the grave: the coals thereof *are* coals of fire, *which hath* a most vehement flame.

Darby Bible Translation: Set me as a seal upon thy heart, As a seal upon thine arm: For love is strong as death; Jealousy is cruel as Sheol: The flashes thereof are flashes of fire, Flames of Jah.

World English Bible: Set me as a seal on your heart, as a seal on your arm; for love is strong as death. Jealousy is as cruel as Sheol. Its flashes are flashes of fire, a very flame of Yahweh.

Young's Literal Translation: Set me as a seal on thy heart, as a seal on thine arm, For strong as death is love, Sharp as Sheol is jealousy, Its burnings are burnings of fire, a flame of Jah!

American Standard Version: Set me as a seal upon thy heart, As a seal upon thine arm: For love is strong as death; Jealousy is cruel as Sheol; The flashes thereof are flashes of fire, A very flame of Jehovah.

(All are versions of Song of Solomon 8:6)

Simply by reading these different versions, we learn the most amazing truth. The eternal flame of God is love. All consuming love is like the fire enfolding itself in the first chapter of Ezekiel, by giving all its substance. Just as it is written in Song of Solomon 8:7, "Many waters cannot quench love neither can floods drown it: if a man give all the substance of his house for love, it would utterly be contemned [scorned]."

Jesus gave all that He had and was scorned by a death on the cross. Before the foundation of the earth was laid, the Lamb was slain. The end of the story was written before the beginning. Between publishing the first book, *Fire in the Bible,* and working on the manuscript for the second book, I came to the realization that I could not finish this book if I didn't know how it ended. It was then it became apparent the end would be about the eternal flame of God. Song of Solomon 8:6 describes the coals of fire, otherwise translated as the flashes of fire, as having a most vehement flame. Other translations call it the flames of Jah, the very flame of Yahweh, the very flame of Jehovah.

The footnote for that verse in my *Key Word Study Bible* says "a most vehement flame" describes God's power unleashed to its fullest extent when it uses the word Jah in the Hebrew translation. Strong's definition for Jah (numbered 3050) says it is the sacred name of God. Searching the root word for Jah went from the name of God to the name of Judah, the tribe Jesus came from to the name of Joseph, which by coincidence is the name of the earthly father of Jesus. The search continued with the name, Jekuthiel, which means the obedience of God. That name traces its beginnings in the feminine word for foundation and ends with the word that means Almighty strength.

The love that is stronger than death is the resurrection power that brought Jesus back to life. He is so jealous for our love He obediently submitted His divinity to the grave so that we might be delivered from the wages of sin. The eternal flame burns with love unleashed to its fullest extent! No greater love has anyone than he lay down his life for someone. The beauty of His Holiness burns with the brilliance of the eternal flame of His vehemence… His name! Love is the ignited flame of God. This is the fire that burns in the pages of the Bible.

AFTERWORD

MY RECENT FIRE

It's been almost twelve years since I finished the original word study that led to the writing of this book. I praise the Lord for all that He has allowed as my husband and I have gone through our own baptism of fire. At the point where I only had seven verses left in Revelation to finish, I had to get ten stitches in my left index finger. I was amazed to see that I could still type without it. While at the hospital, I was monitored with a pulse rate over 150 then down to 32. I was told to consider having a procedure that would burn part of my heart to correct that problem. My doctor suggested I try a medication instead. The fire continues to burn. Several times through the process of writing this book, I have dealt with depression. I don't view it as many do. I have experienced the closeness of the Lord so intimately during those times. The refining process is life-long. I trust the sovereign purpose of God in all things.

I have received the World Challenge Pulpit Series by David Wilkerson by mail for years, and so many times, his words speak directly to my circumstances. His January 24, 2011 edition ended with the words: "No matter what you are facing, He (the Lord) will not allow Satan to overcome you. He has put a wall of fire around you. And he is ready to come to your aid at a moment's noticed." I needed to be reminded of what the Lord had shown me through the process of writing this book. After all, it was the vision of the Lord in a wall of fire that began my study of the word fire.

It's been several months since I finished the book (or so I thought) but as I struggle through my health issues, I needed to be reminded of God's protection and providence. My faith has faltered through the uncertainty of what is happening to my heart. The medication has made me very tired. I've been angry with God, sad and even distant as I've tried to come to terms with this most recent fire. I know so many are going through their own trial by fire especially my husband who continues to inspire me with his great attitude despite all that he deals with.

It's as if my faith has been eclipsed by fear. I've even thought the Lord was going to take me home because of the intensity, frequency, and severity of my heart beating irregularly. There are several times in Jeremiah that he wrote how the Lord tries the heart and reins. The word reins translates to mean kidneys in the Hebrew. The kidneys control blood pressure so we can understand the connection physically. I've seen both the top and bottom numbers of my blood pressure read in the hundreds along with my heart rate. I've seen some improvement with the medication.

On a spiritual level, I'm searching to understand what I am to learn through this test. If all things work out for good to those who love God and are called to His purpose, then why should I fear and doubt? Just having my heart race makes me feel afraid physically. I've quoted scriptures to myself about casting my cares on Him and having perfect peace, asking the Lord to guard my heart and mind. I've cried out to the Lord for help and felt like He wasn't listening. So when I read the Wilkerson series on "Accusing God of Child Neglect," I was convicted. Knowing that

He knows what I'm going through, knowing that He cares for me and that He is more than able to take care of all that I am going through…I chose to trust His sovereignty. So once again, I need to take all those thoughts captive and not go by my feelings. I know that the Lord will use this for good because He knows I love Him, and He has a purpose in all this and for my future.

REFLECTING JESUS

In a Chicago radio interview about my first book, I was asked about the baptism of fire. I shared the goldsmith knows the gold is purified when he can see his reflection in it. All the fires we face in this life will bring us to the clarity of shining with the glory of God. That's how I saw my husband, John. He had become so incredibly attractive to me. I felt like a teenager in love again as I would just stare at him working around our land or waiting for him to return. He was reflecting Jesus to me. His furnace of affliction was nearing its end and he had fought the good fight while contending for the faith. He received his crown of life and slipped into eternity on a hot desert day in June doing exactly what he loved to do—work. I was privileged to be with him at that most sacred moment when the Lord asked me to release him to Him and I heard John in the spirit say, "Be happy for me, rejoice." In the panic of trying to breathe him back to life and then praying for the Lord's will to be done as the paramedics tried to revive him, I knew he had gone home in glory. I was faintly aware that a song by Chris Rice was on the radio. The lyrics exemplified the moment: With your last heartbeat, kiss the world good-bye and fly away to Jesus. John's trial by fire began about six months after I started studying the word fire in 1997 and I finished the second manuscript about six months before he went home to Jesus.

We had been told almost six months earlier that there was nothing more they could do for his heart. We were trying a new medication because the other one had give him such terrible headaches. We were holding on to hope because we were told that his heart had grown vessels around a blockage but he still had three blockages and it was getting hard for him to do much of anything without using nitro glycerin regularly. But that didn't stop him. On the drive to work that day, he said, "I'm going to go until I drop."

We had just shared lunch in the shade of the carport we were going to turn into a bedroom for our family friends. We had turned some buckets upside down to sit on and ate lunch, then sang along to the song on the radio: You are the Air I Breathe. He got up and as I talked to our friend she screamed, I turned and saw John on the ground. I held him in my arms as I saw the light leave his eye. At that exact moment, he opened his eyes to the glory of God no longer in pain. He is safe in the presence of the Lord and I know I will see him again. This life is a blip on the screen compared to eternity. I have a profound expectation of our reunion. Heaven is more real knowing that John is there and the Lord has shown me a vision of him holding our baby, Joy, who was miscarried in 1996.

With all that John went through, he was bold in sharing his faith; persevered through constant pain, had his moments of anger and frustration but overall would tell you it made him a better man. He was an incredible witness of faith in God even though he did not receive his healing here. With all the close calls, he would tell me if he died I should go forward and stay focused. The most amazing confirmation that I truly did hear John say "Rejoice" in the spirit is that the next day I opened his Bible to look up a scripture and there I found my birthday card. It wasn't signed but it said on the front over a photo of large sunflowers: Rejoice in the Lord, again I say Rejoice.

Sunflowers became a theme for the celebration of his life and continued to appear throughout the summer to all our family in glorious surprising fashion. The year before John had lost his childhood friend to heaven. Before he passed, he had given John some sunflower seeds from a tall one that he had grown. We had planted those seeds together and from them grew the largest sunflower I had ever seen. His last project was to turn our former horse corral into a prayer garden. You bet it will have sunflowers in it. There I will place his ashes. He was so peaceful on our land. So the dust returns to the earth and the spirit returns to God who gave it. I now imagine John helping Jesus build those mansions for all of us.

A PROPHECY

The Lord would say: My fire is coming to those who will submit and trust Me. If you will share in My glory, you must be willing to share in My suffering. My crucifixion was My baptism by fire. Your willingness to become a living sacrifice will be your baptism by fire. This fire will continue the work of sanctification. Remember Daniel's friends in the furnace of fire. I was there. I will be with you in your furnace of fire. Zechariah spoke of the third of my people who will be purified like gold and tried like silver. This is the final remnant church. My people are now being tested individually and some will go on to be tested corporately as this group of saints be purified and made white. Let My perfect love vanquish your fears. The pouring out of My Holy Spirit as the latter rain will sustain My beloved during the persecution and tribulation. The patience of the saints is exercised as the enemy seeks to wear out and overcome them. Know that I will shorten the days for My elect. My prophets have spoken and revealed what will transpire. My Word clarifies My Word. The end times herald the new heaven and new earth where I will dwell with My people for all eternity in perfection. Do not lose your hope for the day when I will make all things new. In My presence is fullness of joy. Intimacy with Me, the Father, Son, and Holy Spirit is found in Our Holy Fire. My Word reveals this. My love is the eternal flame that burns to light the New Jerusalem. Let My love consume you. You are my bride. This baptism of fire is burning to bring you to perfection. Embrace it in total abandon until your love for me is burning in My eternal flame.

I am so grateful for the urging of the Holy Spirit that brought this work to completion. To God Be the Glory!

Jesus Rules,
Lily

BIBLIOGRAPHY

1. *King James Bible*. Cambridge, 1769.
2. Davis, John D. *A Dictionary of the Bible*. Philadelphia: Westminster, 1921.
3. Zodhiates, Spiros. *Hebrew-Greek Key Word Study Bible*. King James Version ed. AMG Publisher, 1991.
4. Cruden, Alexander. *Cruden's Compact Concordance*. Zondervan Publishing House, 1970.
5. Biblos.com: Matthew Henry's Commentary and Wycliffe Bible Commentary.
6. http://www.kerryr.net/pioneers/binary.htm.
7. David Wilkerson's Times Square Newsletter, January 12, 2011 Edition.
8. Cheryl Bear's Lyrics.
9. Conversations on Eschatology with Pat Lutz.